Waking Up Slowly

WAKING UP SLOWLY

*Spiritual lessons from my dog, my kids, critters,
and other unexpected places*

Dave Burchett

TYNDALE
MOMENTUM™

*The nonfiction imprint of
Tyndale House Publishers, Inc.*

Visit Tyndale online at www.tyndale.com.

Visit Tyndale Momentum online at www.tyndalemomentum.com.

TYNDALE, *Tyndale Momentum*, and Tyndale's quill logo are registered trademarks of Tyndale House Publishers, Inc. The Tyndale Momentum logo is a trademark of Tyndale House Publishers, Inc. Tyndale Momentum is the nonfiction imprint of Tyndale House Publishers, Inc., Carol Stream, Illinois.

Waking Up Slowly: Spiritual Lessons from My Dog, My Kids, Critters, and Other Unexpected Places

Designed by Julie Chen

Edited by Bonne Steffen

Published in association with the literary agency of D.C. Jacobson & Associates LLC, an Author Management Company. www.dcjacobson.com.

For information about special discounts for bulk purchases, please contact Tyndale House Publishers at csresponse@tyndale.com or call 800-323-9400.

ISBN 978-1-4964-1582-0

Printed in the United States of America

23	22	21	20	19	18	17
7	6	5	4	3	2	1

To Joni.

How can I say thank you for all you have done? Your love has been my constant through a lot of trials. I cannot imagine what my life would have been without you. Thank you for your patience, persistence, and prayer. You certainly needed an abundance of all of those to live with me. I am so grateful we fought through our valleys and emerged hand in hand. I appreciate you more every year I am blessed to be at your side. This book is for you. For us. We made it together, and I would not have wanted it any other way.

I love you.

Contents

Introduction

A NUMBER OF MY BOOK IDEAS end up in a Dumpster, but I never dreamed I would find a book idea standing next to one! The television trailers where I direct major-league baseball games are located well outside the beautifully manicured grass of the Texas Rangers' home field and near the containers that collect the daily garbage of forty thousand baseball fans. I live a glamorous life.

In that unlikely place I saw the unmistakable smile of my friend Mike as he walked toward me. "I am so glad to see you!" I said, giving him a hug. It was the first time I had seen Mike since his detox from prescription-pill addiction. We had been walking together through his life-and-death battle with these drugs. In fact, he read an early version of my previous book *Stay* during his detox agony and found some help in those stories.

"I went to my first Narcotics Anonymous meeting today," Mike said.

"What was that experience like?"

"It was one of the hardest but, at the same time, one of

the best days of my life," he said solemnly. "I stood up and told a room full of strangers that I am an addict."

I listened while he continued to describe the scene.

"When I admitted my addiction, the meeting stopped."

"What do you mean, it stopped?" I asked.

"Every single person in the room walked over to my chair, hugged me, and told me that I was the most important person in the room today."

I felt chills. All of us dream about that kind of community. Every person recognized the importance of Mike taking that painful first step of admitting that he had a problem and he needed help.

But my Dumpster devotion was not finished.

"I looked around the room after that moment of love and affirmation," Mike recounted, "and I realized something sad. In the past, if I had seen many of these same people on the street, I would have made harsh judgments, jokes, or mean comments about their appearance."

That hit my heart. I have been so judgmental of others without taking a moment of my precious time to hear their stories.

Later, I reflected on the remarkable experience my friend had shared. I asked God to open my heart to see how He could teach me through the people I would not normally seek out. God often uses the "least of these" more remarkably than the pretty and powerful. Mike had given me a profound and sacred moment by a Dumpster. I wondered how many times I had stumbled over other sacred moments because I was too self-absorbed to notice.

I am inviting you to my own gathering of need and confession, as I stand and haltingly admit some hard truths about myself.

Hi, my name is Dave, and I am proud, hypocritical, and judg-mental. I am addicted to praise. I get distracted by the insignificant and stub my toe on the sacred every day without noticing. If you can stand, smile kindly, and shout out, "Hi, Dave," then we may have some things to learn together on this journey. You are the most important person in the room right now. Let's learn together how to enjoy God and one another more fully in the moment.

The Premise: Living More Fully

For the threescore years and some change that I have been on this planet, I have operated like the George Harrison lyric, "If you don't know where you're going, any road will take you there." Of course, I have a daily to-do list. I make regular plans to advance my career and for my family's activities. But every morning I wake up and basically let daily circum-stances affect my mood, my productivity, and my happiness. I suspect I am not alone in that routine.

If only I took my cue from my rescued Labrador friend, Maggie, who can capture a playful moment at the drop of a hat—er, toy. Just now, Maggie walked through the room, spotted her red, oversize squeaky bone, leapt through the air to grab it, and started a game. *That* is living in the moment.

Maggie's ability to live fully and joyfully in the moment amuses and even inspires me. The sad reality is that I dismiss my canine friend's talent to enjoy each moment. I rationalize her skill as entirely due to a lack of a calendar, a smartphone, and a spouse or significant other. I write it off as a cute canine characteristic, but certainly not practical for her human liv-ing in this crazy world full of diversions and expectations.

But is that true? Is my slavish addiction to performance, attention, and (gasp) devices robbing me of the joy, smiles, kindness, and affirmation that my heavenly Father desires for me—and for all of us—to enjoy each day? Is my frustration that I can't catch my breath long enough to enjoy this journey just another ugly lie from Satan, hoping to rob me of the very intimacy with God that I desperately need?

We live in the most connected culture in the history of the world, but it's arguably the most disconnected from God and one another. So today I embark on a journey to intentionally live more fully in the moment and to be more connected to God, others, and myself. It is a journey that I have started many times before, like a New Year's Day fitness program. After the death of a dear friend, I vowed to live more fully each day. When my wife, Joni, transitioned from cancer patient to survivor, I promised myself to take nothing for granted. Inevitably, I allow the hectic pace of life to blur my focus, and then I forget my resolve.

Is this goal even possible to achieve? Can a very old dog learn a pretty radical new trick to live more consistently in the moment?

If you have read more than a few words of my humble ramblings, you know that I am a Christian and that this worldview defines my writing. So my first step was to see if there is a biblical rationale for my little experiment.

I researched what God's Word has to say about living for this day. Reformer Martin Luther's favorite psalm provides one insight:

> This is the day the LORD has made.
>   We will rejoice and be glad in it.
> PSALM 118:24

That seems pretty straightforward. The Lord has given us today. What do we do with that gift?

Solomon offered this wisdom in Ecclesiastes:

It is good for people to eat, drink, and enjoy their work
under the sun during the short life God has given them,
and to accept their lot in life. And it is a good thing to
receive wealth from God and the good health to enjoy it.
To enjoy your work and accept your lot in life—this is
indeed a gift from God. God keeps such people so busy
enjoying life that they take no time to brood over the past.
ECCLESIASTES 5:18-20

Jesus weighed in on the mistake of allowing tomorrow's
worries to rob you of joy today:

Don't worry about tomorrow, for tomorrow will bring
its own worries. Today's trouble is enough for today.
MATTHEW 6:34

The psalmist (likely David), Solomon, and Jesus endorsed
the idea of living fully and intentionally present in each day.
That is a pretty solid list of references, in my opinion.

Philosophically, the idea of living more fully in the
moment is grand and noble. But practically, it seems impossible. Is God really there? Does He care about my mundane
daily activities? Does He know me? Does He reveal Himself
through creation and creatures?

Every time I begin thinking that way, I turn to Psalm 139,
one of the most inspiring passages of Scripture written by
David. We don't know when he wrote this stirring account of
God's indescribable attributes. Some scholars believe David
wrote it when he was a shepherd, composing it while gazing
at the stars and the vastness of the heavens. Some think he

wrote it when he became king over Israel. As a more experienced human myself (that is PC for "old"), it certainly feels like David had to have lived a little more life in order to write such a majestic description of God. The words are intensely personal as David makes three observations about the greatness of God versus his own finiteness:

> God knows everything about me.
> God is everywhere I am.
> God ordains everything about me.

If those statements about God are true, then it should change how I go about my daily business.

The psalmist writes that God knows my every move and thought. And I was concerned about the government snooping on me!

> GOD, investigate my life;
>   get all the facts firsthand.
> **I'm an open book to you;**
>   even from a distance, you know what
>   I'm thinking.
> You know when I leave and when I get back;
>   I'm never out of your sight.
> You know everything I'm going to say
>   before I start the first sentence.
> I look behind me and you're there,
>   then up ahead and you're there, too—
>   your reassuring presence, coming and going.
> This is too much, too wonderful—
>   I can't take it all in!
> PSALM 139:1-6, MSG (EMPHASIS ADDED)

I don't know about you, but that is incredibly daunting to me. I think and do a lot of things that I would prefer to keep in Las Vegas mode. But David is saying the idea of a "secret sin" is a fool's concept. I am known by my Creator, and I am pursued by Him.

> Is there anyplace I can go to avoid your Spirit?
>   to be out of your sight?
> If I climb to the sky, you're there!
>   If I go underground, you're there!
> If I flew on morning's wings
>   to the far western horizon,
> You'd find me in a minute—
>   you're already there waiting!
>
> PSALM 139:7-10, MSG

There are no secrets from God. There is no hiding from God. My desire to keep those secrets and to hide from His presence comes from a false belief that God would love me less when I sin. The uniqueness of grace for a follower of Christ is that God already knows everything about me (and you), and He loves us exactly the same on our best or worst day.

Don't rush past that truth for Christians. Read it again.

God knows everything about you, and *He loves you exactly the same on your best or worst day.*

The psalmist goes on to clearly proclaim that none of us is an accident, even if your parents might have said exactly that!

> You know me inside and out,
>   you know every bone in my body;
> You know exactly how I was made, bit by bit,
>   how I was sculpted from nothing into something.

> Like an open book, you watched me grow from
>   conception to birth;
>   all the stages of my life were spread out before you,
>   **The days of my life all prepared**
>   before I'd even lived one day.
> PSALM 139:15-16, MSG (EMPHASIS ADDED)

That is a difficult idea to wrap my finite mind around. I am writing these words before Christmas, a time of year when I faithfully watch *It's a Wonderful Life*. That classic movie reminds me that I am here for a reason, despite falling short of the dreams I once had. I once envisioned I would direct a World Series and maybe even write a bestseller. Remember the exuberant dreams that George Bailey shared with his soon-to-be wife, Mary? He had his life planned out and knew exactly how it would look.

> "Mary. I know what I'm gonna do tomorrow and
> the next day and next year and the year after that.
> I'm shaking the dust of this crummy little town off
> my feet and I'm gonna see the world! Italy, Greece,
> the Parthenon . . . the Colosseum. Then I'm coming
> back here and go to college to see what they know,
> and then I'm gonna build things. I'm gonna build
> airfields. I'm gonna build skyscrapers a hundred
> stories high. I'm gonna build bridges a mile long."[1]

None of that happened. George Bailey's dreams had to be put aside to support his family. He lived a successful but humdrum life that fell apart when his uncle Billy lost a huge amount of money on his way to deposit it in the bank. The family business was about to go bankrupt, something that would dramatically impact or even ruin the entire community. There seemed to be no hope, and George wished that he had never lived.

And then an awkward angel named Clarence (probably like the one I would get assigned) shows him what would have happened if that wish had come true. What if God had not put George Bailey in Bedford Falls? You likely know the rest of the story. George sees how many people and events his seemingly banal existence had changed for the good. His actions had even led to saving dozens of lives.

Clarence makes this simple but profound observation: "Strange, isn't it? Each man's life touches so many other lives. When he isn't around, he leaves an awful hole, doesn't he?"

Indeed.

The movie powerfully illustrates the truth of Psalm 139: I am known by God. I am watched over by God. I am ordained by God to fulfill a part of His plan. You are not an accident, and neither am I. The apostle Paul shares the amazing truth that we have a preordained reason to be here.

> It's in Christ that we find out who we are and what we are living for. Long before we first heard of Christ and got our hopes up, he had his eye on us, had designs on us for glorious living, part of the overall purpose he is working out in everything and everyone.
>
> EPHESIANS 1:11-12, MSG

I am an important part of the redemptive plan of Christ, and so are you. Every day we have the potential to do something or learn something that will alter someone's life and even eternity. What an amazing thought that God can use someone like me for His purpose. I find that to be a remarkable example of His grace. Our goal is to make that more real in our daily experiences.

The Promise: Realizing God Is Here

God's sense of humor is evident in the timing of this introduction. The political season is now in full force, and writing about promises in this environment is the ultimate irony. Author Carolyn Warner said it well: "Years ago, fairy tales all began with 'Once upon a time . . .'—now we know they all begin with 'If I am elected.'" So many sincere folks passionately believe that their candidate will deliver on the promises conveniently tailored to whichever state he or she is currently visiting.

Not much has changed over the years. Humorist Will Rogers noted nearly a century ago that "if we got one-tenth of what was promised to us in these acceptance speeches there wouldn't be any inducement to go to heaven." Based on the post-election promise-fulfillment percentage in my lifetime, I still have a lot of inducement to hope for heaven.

And it's not just politicians. I roll my eyes at the exorbitant advertising promises for products. I learned the hard way that movies that promise two hours of nonstop laughs have included most of the funny material in the two-minute trailer. I deal with broken promises every day from service providers (looking at you, cable TV company) and salespeople. I have endured broken promises in relationships that left me with emotional scars and a wariness to trust anyone's word.

Some of us have been taught by preachers that God will be our personal ATM if we have the right amount of faith. But that faith works only if it is combined with a donation to said preacher's personal retirement or corporate jet fund. I don't think I am overstating the facts when I say this heresy has been devastating to millions.

Frankly, I suspect we have promise fatigue before we even consider the biblical promises of God. But His promises are different. God does not disappoint, fall short, forget, get tired, grumpy, or befuddled. For this journey we are about to begin, I think it is important to lay the foundation.

Recently, Joni and I had an engineer inspect our home's structural integrity. The extreme heat along with the expanding and contracting Texas clay can cause a home to shift and crack, resulting in repairs that can cost thousands and thousands of dollars and often are not permanent. When the engineer finished the inspection, we held our breath for the verdict.

"Your foundation is in great shape. The contractor built your home on piers that distribute the stress and are anchored in bedrock."

That sounded like a pretty good approach for this project. Is this pursuit of finding God more consistently anchored on the bedrock, foundational promises of His Word? And if I am going to invest intentional effort in finding God in everyday moments, I must feel confident that God's location setting is always on.

In the Old Testament book of Jeremiah there are a couple of often-overlooked verses that follow the familiar passage about God knowing and having good plans for us (see Jeremiah 29:11). Here is what God says next:

In those days when you pray, **I will listen.** If you look for me wholeheartedly, **you will find me.**
JEREMIAH 29:12-13 (EMPHASIS ADDED)

That is a pretty cool combo platter. God knows us. He has a plan for us. That plan offers hope for the future. He listens. And He is available.

God also tells us that His love will not fade like romantic love or other relational love sometimes does.

> Give thanks to the LORD, for he is good!
>   His faithful love endures forever.
>
> 1 CHRONICLES 16:34

God does not promise that everything will be perfect. Far from it. You and I are pretty much guaranteed to have some degree of suffering; none of us gets out of this life unscathed. Here is what God does promise:

> He comforts us in all our troubles so that we can comfort others. When they are troubled, we will be able to give them the same comfort God has given us. For the more we suffer for Christ, the more God will shower us with his comfort through Christ.
>
> 2 CORINTHIANS 1:4-5

The idea of suffering for Christ does not get people to buy prayer cloths, miracle water, and books. However, God's promise to shower me with comfort should give me confidence that I can make it through trials. I have had the opportunity to test this supernatural comfort after the death of our daughter, Katie, from a terminal birth condition, and during the cancer battle Joni fought and won. I can attest that His comfort is real and remarkable.

God's greatest promise of all is salvation to all who believe in His Son.

> I am not ashamed of this Good News about Christ. It is the power of God at work, saving everyone who

believes—the Jew first and also the Gentile. This Good News tells us how God makes us right in his sight. This is accomplished from start to finish by faith. As the Scriptures say, "It is through faith that a righteous person has life."

ROMANS 1:16-17

God promised that I am secure forever when I placed my trust in the finished work of Christ. This was a big one for a recovering legalist who had been taught otherwise early in my faith journey.

I give them eternal life, and **they will never perish. No one** can snatch them away from me.

JOHN 10:28 (EMPHASIS ADDED)

God promises to meet our needs. This is a tough one for us. We are culturally conditioned to pray for wants, bombarded by messages that tell us this car or that product or that promotion will make us happy. God promises only that He will give us all we need.

Seek the Kingdom of God above all else, and live righteously, and he will give you **everything you need.**

MATTHEW 6:33 (EMPHASIS ADDED)

This may be one of the most common places where I stub my toe on something sacred without even knowing it, because I am looking for some glorious blessing. A common provision of grace is at my feet, and I walk right over it. Part of the challenge for me will be reorienting my thinking about what really matters.

After His resurrection, Jesus gave final instructions to His followers, telling them to make disciples and to baptize those new believers in the name of the Father, Son, and Holy Spirit. And then He says,

> Be sure of this: I am with you always, even to the end of the age.
> MATTHEW 28:20

We often talk about the importance of last words and the weight they carry. These last recorded words of Jesus are so encouraging. Christ wanted us to be sure that He was going to be present with us for every earthly breath we take.

I don't live as if I believe that promise. I feel alone so often, struggling with doubts. Part of this journey is to learn to trust the truth that He is always with me. I choose to plant my flag of belief on that hill as we start this adventure. And I choose to believe this truth that our Lord proclaimed in the Gospel of John:

> I have loved you even as the Father has loved me.
> Remain in my love.
> JOHN 15:9

God is with us every moment. He knows our every thought. He listens to our prayers. And He has promised us that if we seek Him wholeheartedly we *will* find Him. That is the premise and the promise. Let's look at the process to become more connected to God and one another.

The Process: Removing the Distractions
A vital part of this process will be to disconnect from the devices that enslave me. I will need to examine the actions

and attitudes that cause me to be distracted and lose sight of what matters. To be perfectly honest, I feel ill equipped to be your tour guide on this journey.

But then I think about how God works. He works through the unexpected and the unlikely people. Big check mark there.

The truth is that if I can do this, I can almost guarantee you can. I have never felt more convicted about my specific weakness of distractedness than I do in approaching this project.

My brain was not wired to factory specs, and that has been a problem all my life. My educational background was, to be very kind, inconsistent. I had an attention deficit before it was "cool." Instead of undergoing testing and receiving medication, I was called into the guidance counselor's office and chastised for underachievement and laziness. Those are indeed great motivators.

Recently, a high school friend of mine sent me a message that made me chuckle. Jane wrote that she was enjoying my books and blog. "Your teachers at Chillicothe High School would have been very proud of you," she kindly wrote. I hope they would be proud, but I can guarantee you they would first be surprised!

At any rate, I survived high school with good enough grades to pass, and I enrolled in Marietta College with a determination to show I could do well academically. I stayed interested for one semester and did well enough to make the desired dean's list. After proving I could accomplish that goal, my interest promptly turned to Ping-Pong, pinball, and Strat-O-Matic baseball for the second semester. Not surprisingly, I dropped out after my freshman year to become a disc jockey. It was a well-thought-out strategy.

So here are my credentials put on the table:

College dropout
Marginal Ping-Pong player
1972 high game on the Play Ball pinball machine—
    Student Center, Marietta College

Not exactly Algonquin Round Table material. I would have loved embellishing the old academic credentials. But it was like my grandpa used to say when he noted that you can't polish a—uhhh, well, never mind what my grandpa used to say.

I found my refuge in reading and research. I learned that you never stop learning. And something incredible happened in my life—I realized the miracle of how God can use anyone, even a slacker like me. Getting puffed up with pride is not an option for me when it comes to my academic credentials, so I lean fully on God's grace for this journey.

> "My grace is all you need. My power works best
> in weakness." So now I am glad to boast about
> my weaknesses, so that the power of Christ can
> work through me. That's why I take pleasure in my
> weaknesses, and in the insults, hardships, persecutions,
> and troubles that I suffer for Christ. For when I am
> weak, then I am strong.
>
> 2 CORINTHIANS 12:9-10

I have seen how God is faithful when I trust Him. So if you can relate to a fumbling, bumbling mess who is still trying to figure all this out, then you might be in the right place. Together we can see how God can meet us in our personal weaknesses and impart His strength.

Ahead, you will find twenty-one chapters with stories and Scripture that address the actions and attitudes that keep us from connecting with God, each other, and even ourselves. At the end of each chapter, I have included a Scripture—"God's Take"—and a suggested action—"A Dose of Grace"—for reflection. You may choose to write down the lessons and insights you glean from this adventure.

Whether or not you choose to implement the actions is entirely your call. There is no grading and no condemnation. This is about getting more connected to God and one another.

You can establish your own routine for this quest, but this is what I plan to do. I will not check my smartphone for the first hour after I wake up. Instead, I will spend that time reading Scripture or listening to messages or music that feed my soul. I will schedule my social media time for the day.

I have also crafted a prayer that I will recite first thing in the morning to get my mind focused. Since these words will be spoken before my first sip of coffee, I will print this on a card just in case my mind refuses to boot up properly without caffeine.

Good morning, God.

I believe that You know everything about me. I believe that You are everywhere that I am. I believe that You have a purpose for my life and for this day. I pray that You will show me Your presence today. I pray that I will slow down, quiet my mind, open my heart and eyes, and look for a postcard from You.

I am grateful that because of Jesus I can boldly ask You for tender mercies today, whether it is a day of great joy or profound sadness. I know that whatever my circumstances, You are there. I believe You are all around me. I know because of Your grace that there is nothing I can do to lose Your approval. So would You show me Your kindness, Your beauty, Your power, Your comfort, and Your love today?

I pray this in Jesus' name.

Okay . . . I am not getting any younger. Let's try this!

CHAPTER I

THE CURSE OF CULTURE

And lead us not into temptation,
but deliver us from e-mail.

FIVE-YEAR-OLD STUDENT RECITING
THE LORD'S PRAYER

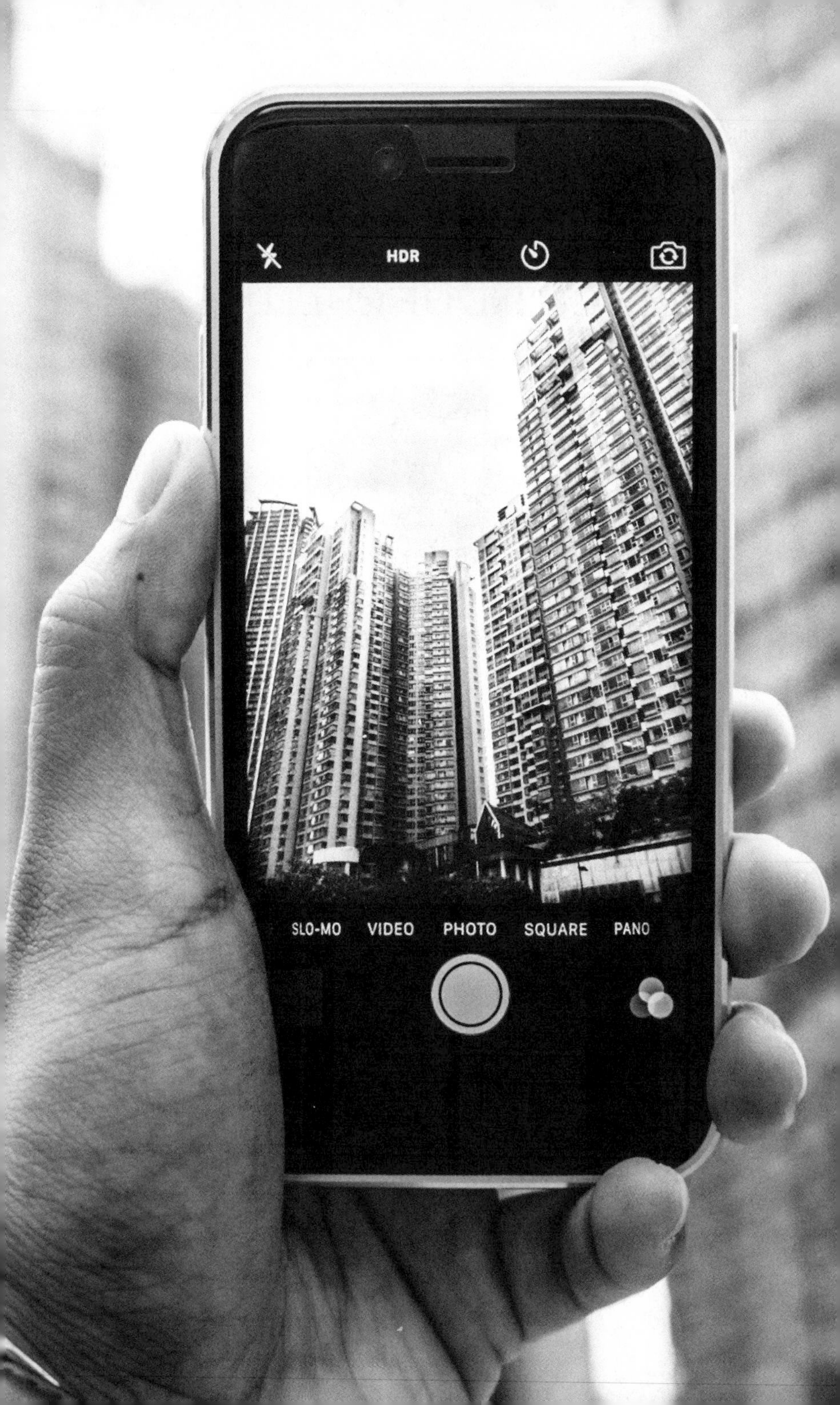
HDR
SLO-MO
VIDEO
PHOTO
SQUARE
PANO

"AND LEAD US NOT into temptation, but deliver us from email." I say amen to that prayer. And, Lord, deliver us from Facebook. Instagram. Twitter. LinkedIn. Snapchat. I remember my beloved looking at me when I announced my plan to limit my smartphone usage. "This is going to be harder than you think," she said encouragingly. She was right.

Recently Joni and I took a trip to the mountains to unwind and regroup. Everything was set for a relaxing getaway. We pulled into an off-site airport parking lot and unloaded the luggage. When the shuttle van approached, I instinctively checked my pocket.

No phone.

"Where is my phone?" I asked reflexively.

"Did you have it earlier?" Joni asked.

"Yes, I know it was in the car."

We started down the typical path that causes me to have to ask for forgiveness later in the day.

"When did you last see it?" Joni quizzed.

"If I remembered where I last saw it, I would go and get it," I responded, with what might have been interpreted as a touch of sarcasm.

Joni rifled through the car and could not find it. I looked under the seat, under the mats, and between the cushions. Nothing. We were traveling with our friends Bob and Judy. Bob called my number, and my Fitbit Bluetooth watch showed that I was receiving a call. The phone was somewhere nearby.

The shuttle driver waited somewhat patiently.

"Go on," we said. "We will get the next one."

Bob called again. Again the Bluetooth watch showed an incoming call. Where was that doggone phone? We searched a bit more frantically now, as our time had dwindled to get to the terminal. Finally, I decided we had to head to the airport sans phone. I felt like I was leaving a man behind in my unit. That I was being a traitor to my trusty sidekick.

When we got through security, I booted up my computer and ran the lost phone app. Sure enough, the phone was located at the parking site. Joni flashed that mischievous smile that can be endearing on other occasions.

"You know this is a God thing," she said.

"Too soon," I replied.

Day one without the phone was awful. I had planned this calculated, me-in-control weaning from the glowing seduction of the device. Now I was cut off without any preparation. Like a person who doesn't think he or she is an alcoholic, until that person ends up in a dry county, I realized I was addicted to this phone and its relentless flirtations for my attention.

Day two was much better. I kind of liked not seeing all the rantings on social media.

By day three, I hardly missed it at all. And I began to notice more fully the impact these devices have on relationships. All around me, people stared at their devices. All I had to look at was the sky and the mountains. I began to watch how these inherently helpful and often good devices sabotage relationships. I would see a family at a table and every single person's eyes were glued to a screen. Couples sat silently, transfixed by their phones.

It took my inability to find my phone to reveal to me that I was way too often that person. By the end of day three I had to confess to Joni that it was indeed a God thing that my phone had played hide-and-seek at the airport. She smiled that smile that all husbands recognize when our brides are right and we are not. That was a very hard sentence to write.

Our culture has information-fatigue syndrome, and Christians are just as infected as the general populace. Three-quarters of adults now use a social-networking site of some kind. The average time spent on those sites is a staggering sixteen minutes per hour. The solution suggested by one publication is a digital detox. That is defined as (and I am not making this up) "a period of time during which a person refrains from using electronic devices so one can focus on social interaction in the physical world."[1]

Whatever happened to talking to people, aka, interacting with flesh-and-blood humans?

We are the most connected culture in history and yet, at the same time, the most disconnected from God and one another. I couldn't get through a dinner without furtively glancing at my smartphone, just in case some important message arrived. There is even a word for the behavior now. When you snub someone because of your phone you are *phubbing*. The Hankamer School of Business at Baylor University did a study of how this phubbing behavior affected romantic relationships. The Baptists have come a long way since the no-dancing days at Baylor!

Researchers James A. Roberts and Meredith E. David have identified eight types of common phubbing:

1. During a typical mealtime that my partner and I spend together, my partner pulls out and checks his or her cell phone.
2. My partner places his or her cell phone where they can see it when we are together.
3. My partner keeps his or her cell phone in their hand when he or she is with me.
4. When my partner's cell phone rings or beeps, he or she pulls it out even if we are in the middle of a conversation.
5. My partner glances at his or her cell phone while talking to me.
6. During leisure time that my partner and I are able to spend together, my partner uses his or her cell phone.
7. My partner uses his or her cell phone when we are out together.
8. If there is a lull in our conversation, my partner will check his or her cell phone.[2]

I admit I try to be sneaky and place my phone in different spots, so I can glance at an important sports score or "vital" text. Joni is not fooled. Surprise. She will occasionally ask me why I keep looking at my crotch. Or I feverishly check my phone while my bride goes to the restroom. What is wrong with me?

And since I am busy making confessions, I will go ahead and own these, too: I have sometimes been distracted during a church service by my smartphone. I have checked my fantasy football lineup while the offering plate is being passed, somehow thinking this is more spiritually okay than checking it during the sermon. That must be covered in Leviticus somewhere.

After reading through the phubbing list, I realized I was guilty of a disturbing eight out of eight infractions. Not surprisingly, the study goes on to discover that phubbing causes conflict and a lower level of satisfaction in a relationship. Right now I am so grateful that God and Joni are both great forgivers.

I have no one to blame but myself, but I want to put some of the blame on our culture that has told me I must respond and respond NOW if I am texted or called. Talk about an anxiety inducer!

For many of us this is a real relational, emotional, and spiritual issue. So how do we reconnect with God and with one other? I believe it begins with a heart and mind transformation. Paul prescribed this to the church at Rome:

> Don't copy the behavior and customs of this world, but let God transform you into a new person by **changing the way you think.** Then you will learn to know God's will for you, which is good and pleasing and perfect.
> ROMANS 12:2 (EMPHASIS ADDED)

I love the way *The Message* fleshes out the process of renewing our minds:

> So here's what I want you to do, God helping you: **Take your everyday, ordinary life—your sleeping, eating,**

going-to-work, and walking-around life—and place it before God as an offering. Embracing what God does for you is the best thing you can do for him. Don't become so well-adjusted to your culture that you fit into it without even thinking. **Instead, fix your attention on God. You'll be changed from the inside out.** Readily recognize what he wants from you, and quickly respond to it. Unlike the culture around you, always dragging you down to its level of immaturity, God brings the best out of you, develops well-formed maturity in you.

ROMANS 12:1-2, MSG (EMPHASIS ADDED)

I want that. Really I do. But for me, one obstacle to living this out is how I routinely take things for granted. Anytime I "use, accept, or treat in a careless or indifferent manner"[3] something of value in my life, I am guilty. I don't intend to do that. I don't think that is intentional for most of us. But it will take intentional focus to notice those overlooked little blessings. The definition continues: "to accept without question or objection; assume."[4] Yes, when I take something for granted, which I do almost every day, I assume that thing will always be there.

The better response would be to take a moment to thank God for the little things I rarely think about. Things like clean water and abundant, safe food supplies. When was the last time I thought about that? How about hot water for my shower? I appreciated it only when the hot-water tank ran out.

G. K. Chesterton had the right idea when he penned these words:

You say grace before meals. All right. But I say
grace before the concert and the opera, and grace

before the play and pantomime, and grace before I open a book, and grace before sketching, painting, swimming, fencing, boxing, walking, playing, dancing and grace before I dip the pen in the ink.

Thank God for every seemingly mundane, good thing that comes your way today. A hot cup of coffee or tea. A green light on your commute. A warm (or cool) car to get you to work or school. A favorite song playing. Laughter. A smile from a friend or stranger. A tasty treat. A cuddly dog. A beautiful tree or flower. A blue sky. What is your list of small and overlooked daily mercies?

Today I will remind myself of this simple truth: *The things I take for granted, countless others are longing to receive.* As you focus on that truth, I think you will be amazed at how much work you and I need to do.

GOD'S TAKE

Don't copy the behavior and customs of this world, but let God transform you into a new person by changing the way you think. Then you will learn to know God's will for you, which is good and pleasing and perfect.

ROMANS 12:2

A DOSE OF GRACE

This grace suggestion has two steps. The first is to mute and limit the devices you use. (I never said this would be easy.) Strive to be less obsessed with devices, texts, and messaging. Untethering from our devices for at least a few minutes a day will give us the clarity for the next step—to be aware of every simple blessing that we generally overlook. When you disconnect from your device for a few minutes a day, you begin rewiring your brain. If you're like me and need to write ideas down to remember them, you might want to jot down your insights in a notebook.

CHAPTER 2

HOW TO REVERSE STINKIN' THINKIN'

God has committed himself, ever since creation, to working through his creatures—in particular, through his image-bearing human beings—but they have all let Him down.

N. T. WRIGHT

OUR HOME IS A WELCOMING PLACE to grandkids and grand-dogs alike. One day we were watching Bailey, our ten-year-old golden retriever granddog from the Waco division of Burchett Incorporated. She is a regal and beautiful girl who loves to swim. We took our Maggie and Bailey out to the pool to do just that. Maggie swims like she is competing for the final Olympic-team spot. She goes full bore to the end, jumps out, shakes off, and runs back to the start.

In contrast, Bailey swims to cool off and relax. She will go to the deep-end step and just hang out for minutes at a time. While she was standing there, we noticed Bailey's epically failed attempt to accomplish a common canine task. She watched Maggie shake off water as she exited the pool.

Bailey knew that she needed to do likewise, since this is covered in the dog manual. So she aggressively shook her body.

What she failed to take into account was that she was standing shoulder deep in water. The net effect of her efforts was exactly zero water removed. But that didn't keep her from trying. Periodically she would shake with the same non-results. I smiled at Joni. No matter how often or how violently Bailey shook her body, nothing was going to change unless she changed her position.

I thought about Bailey's failed attempts as I mused about how we as a community of believers need to change how we approach our desire to shake off the crippling effects of this culture on our faith walk. Like Bailey, we need to change our position.

I have said for years that America is one of the toughest places on the planet to be a transformational Christian. You combine material abundance with a constant diet of bad cultural messaging, and you have terrible soil for spiritual growth.

Advertising targets my worst instincts. My happiness is defined by possessions, power, appearance, and experiences. I am encouraged to chase the next thing that will make me happy. After many years of futile pursuit, I have learned this is just more *stinkin' thinkin'*, an actual psychological term.

Stinking thinking is "a bad way of thinking, that makes you believe you will fail, that bad things will happen to you, or that you are not a very good person."[1] That pretty much describes my junior high experience.

We all fall victim to stinkin' thinkin', but it is particularly distressing for a follower of Christ. Christians feel an even bigger sense of failure. They think, *If I can muster up more faith, prayer, study, or general busyness for Jesus, I can overcome this malady, right?* Busyness and wrong thinking lead to tiredness and shame.

Clinical psychiatrist and bestselling author David Burns came up with an excellent checklist of stinkin' thinkin' symptoms:

1. **All-or-nothing thinking**—You see things in black-or-white categories. If a situation falls short of perfect, you see it as a total failure.
2. **Overgeneralization**—You see a single negative event, such as a romantic rejection or a career reversal, as a never-ending pattern of defeat by using words such as "always" or "never" when you think about it.
3. **Mental filter**—You pick out a single negative detail and dwell on it exclusively.
4. **Discounting the positive**—You reject positive experiences by insisting they "don't count." If you do a good job, you may tell yourself that it wasn't good enough or that anyone could have done as well.
5. **Jumping to conclusions**—You interpret things negatively when there are no facts to support your conclusion.
6. **Magnification**—You exaggerate the importance of your problems and shortcomings, or you minimize the importance of your desirable qualities.
7. **Emotional reasoning**—You assume that your negative emotions necessarily reflect the way things really are.
8. **"Should" statements**—You tell yourself that things *should* be the way you hoped or expected them to be.
9. **Labeling**—Labeling is an extreme form of all-or-nothing thinking. Instead of saying "I made a

mistake," you attach a negative label to yourself:
"I'm a loser." You might also label yourself "a fool"
or "a failure" or "a jerk." Labeling is quite irrational
because you are not the same as what you do.
Human beings exist, but "fools," "losers," and "jerks"
do not.

10. **Personalization and blame**—Personalization occurs
when you hold yourself personally responsible for an
event that isn't entirely under your control.[2]

I sincerely hope you are doing better on this checklist
than I am. This is a secular list of bad thinking processes. As
a Christian, I believe that I get the added bonus of spiritual
battle with an enemy that probes my weaknesses constantly
and effectively. This enemy goes by a couple of names. *Satan*
is the Hebrew word that means "adversary," and *devil* comes
from the Greek word *diablos*, which means "false accuser."
Combine these names, and you get an accurate scouting
report: lying enemy.

Many followers of Jesus marginalize the existence of this
enemy in their midst. I'll admit that over the years I have
made jokes about Satan and chuckled at caricatures of the
devil with a pitchfork and horns. But this enemy is not a
Saturday Night Live bit. Jesus took Satan seriously, and if I
am a follower of Christ, then I must as well.

Other Christians seem to believe that Satan is behind
every single negative thing that happens in their lives. That
belief is just as dangerous. Sometimes the bad things that
happen are just the result of life on a fallen planet.

Satan tested Jesus by offering Him everything this world
could give, if Jesus would agree to bow down and worship
His adversary.

"I will give it all to you," he said, "if you will kneel down and worship me."

"Get out of here, Satan," Jesus told him. "For the Scriptures say,

'You must worship the LORD your God and serve only him.'"

Then the devil went away, and angels came and took care of Jesus.

MATTHEW 4:9-11

The apostle Peter underscores the devil's power:

Stay alert! Watch out for your great enemy, the devil. He prowls around like a roaring lion, looking for someone to devour. Stand firm against him, and be strong in your faith. Remember that your family of believers all over the world is going through the same kind of suffering you are.

I PETER 5:8-9

But Peter also gives the secret defense strategy on how to defeat him:

So humble yourselves under the mighty power of God, and at the right time he will lift you up in honor. Give all your worries and cares to God, for he cares about you.

I PETER 5:6-7

Humility is a pretty rare commodity in this selfie-mad culture. Humbling myself before God is an act of strength and not weakness. And I would suggest that giving my worries to God gives Satan precious little room to plant his lies in my heart.

I have to admit that I am afflicted with some degree of stinkin' thinkin'. We need only harken back one chapter to the story of the misplaced phone. After I couldn't find the phone, all of my buttons were pushed. The voices started. *I am stupid. Disorganized.* I remember muttering, "What is wrong with me?" as we pulled away. Joni's questions shamed me, although there was no hint of shame in her tone. This was not about her or a lost phone. There is a spiritual war happening with an enemy who delights in my doubt and shame. The culture contributes a tsunami of unbiblical images and words. How can I overcome this daunting challenge?

Paul has the perfect antidote to stinkin' thinkin' in his letter to the church at Philippi. The letter is written to encourage believers living in a culture that was often hostile to faith, not unlike the times we live in now.

Paul penned this uplifting missive of hope while he was suffering for his faith in a Roman prison. But Paul did not let his circumstances defeat him, and he did not want the Philippians to lose their joy because of opposition.

> Always be full of joy in the Lord. I say it again—rejoice! Let everyone see that you are considerate in all you do. Remember, the Lord is coming soon. Don't worry about anything; instead, pray about everything. Tell God what you need, and thank him for all he has done. Then you will experience God's peace, which exceeds anything we can understand. His peace will guard your hearts and minds as you live in Christ Jesus.
>
> PHILIPPIANS 4:4-7

Those are wonderful words for sure, but then Paul gets to the kicker in the next verse, pinpointing what can stand up against (or take down?) stinkin' thinkin'.

Fix your thoughts on what is true, and honorable, and right, and pure, and lovely, and admirable. Think about things that are excellent and worthy of praise.
PHILIPPIANS 4:8

That is holy positive thinking! Write that reminder on a card. Make it the wallpaper on your device. Write it on the palm of your hand. Stick it on a mirror or the refrigerator. Do whatever you need to do, in order to have these words handy when you find your mind drifting toward stinkin' thinkin'.

I love how *The Message* unpacks this even more:

Summing it all up, friends, I'd say **you'll do best by filling your minds and meditating on things true, noble, reputable, authentic, compelling, gracious— the best, not the worst; the beautiful, not the ugly; things to praise, not things to curse.**
PHILIPPIANS 4:8, MSG (EMPHASIS ADDED)

Today, consider how you will pivot from false accusations to truth. How you plan to switch your thoughts from negative to noble, from angry to gracious. How you can consider the best and not the worst. If you feel moved to do so, record the beautiful and throw out the ugly. Write down your praise.

This is one of the core themes for this journey. It is a hard process, but we have a pretty good support system and a 24-7 help line with no wait times. Today, be aware of your thoughts. Repeat Philippians 4:8 aloud every time your mental GPS suggests the low road.

GOD'S TAKE

Fix your thoughts on what is true, and honorable, and right, and pure, and lovely, and admirable. Think about things that are excellent and worthy of praise.

PHILIPPIANS 4:8

A DOSE OF GRACE

Identify any negative thoughts, images, or ideas you have. Then replace them with your reflections on the encounters, feelings, relationships, and moments today that are true, honorable, right, pure, lovely, and admirable. Carry Philippians 4:8 with you and read it throughout the day. I think you might be surprised at the power of this word of grace as an antidote to stinkin' thinkin'.

CHAPTER 3

BUSYNESS IS NOT
NEXT TO GODLINESS

Jesus is coming soon . . . try and look busy.

BUMPER STICKER

I WAS THINKING ABOUT the sad humor in that bumper sticker when I heard a thump. Then another thump.

It was silent for a few moments so I went back to my writing.

Thump!

Okay, now I had to investigate. What I found was a beautiful male cardinal flying around one of our windows. He would hover near the window and then peck aggressively at the pane.

Thump!

He fluttered around some more and then thumped the glass!

The very focused bird stayed busy for several minutes repeating this odd behavior.

Joni and I had admired a pair of cardinals nesting in a tree just over our back fence for several weeks, but this was new. I did some research and found that cardinals are very territorial. This beautiful bird apparently was seeing his own reflection in the window, and he was letting that intruder know he was not welcome!

We are investigating some ways to reduce the reflection so he can go about the business of raising little cardinals and allowing us to enjoy his gorgeous plumage. I worried that he was going to hurt himself defending his family against a nonexistent threat.

How often do we wear ourselves out and even beat ourselves up trying to defend our "territory"? Invariably, our busyness is generated to counter imagined threats or a need to prove our worth.

We are often button-bustin' proud of how busy we are! Somehow being busy has become an indication of significance and value. If you are not busy, you are not worthy.

A *New York Times* op-ed by Tim Kreider offered this thought-provoking analysis: "Busyness serves as a kind of existential reassurance, a hedge against emptiness; obviously your life cannot possibly be silly or trivial or meaningless if you are so busy, completely booked, in demand every hour of the day."[1]

Busyness as a hedge against emptiness. That is a brilliant synopsis of our need to appear busy and feel needed. Kreider concluded that "it's not as if any of us wants to live like this; it's something we collectively force one another to do."[2]

All of us are adding to that pressure every day. Christians are just as caught up in busyness.

The *Christian Post* reports that in data collected from more than 20,000 Christians in 139 countries (though mostly in America) and between the ages of 15 and 88, "more than 4 in 10 Christians around the world say they 'often' or 'always' rush from task to task. About 6 in 10 Christians say that it's 'often' or 'always' true that 'the busyness of life gets in the way of developing my relationship with God.'"[3]

The survey also found that "by profession, pastors were most likely to say they rush from task to task (54 percent), which adversely affects their relationship with God (65 percent)."[4]

What a tragedy that the pastoral shepherds we hope will show us the way are also caught in scheduling pressure. I don't mean to throw pastors under the bus. The church community puts such unrealistic expectations on pastors to be available 24-7, visit every sick person, spend forty hours on a kick-donkey sermon, and have a perfectly adjusted family. Just typing those expectations made me tired.

Letting my busyness get in the way of my relationship with God shows how out of balance I have let my schedule become.

Nowhere in Scripture will I find this command: be busy, and know that I am God.

My busyness does not please God. My faith pleases Him. And I can't have faith and trust in someone I am too busy to know. Day in and day out, I need to heed this truth:

Be still, and know that I am God.
PSALM 46:10

Solomon wrote about the wisdom of knowing when to let up.

Don't wear yourself out trying to get rich.
    Be wise enough to know when to quit.
PROVERBS 23:4

I have a remarkable role model for how to balance busy-ness and priorities. Jesus never allowed the tyranny of the urgent to supersede the ultimately more important reward of relationships. He didn't feel the need to drive Himself to exhaustion to teach and preach.

> Then, leaving the crowds outside, Jesus went into the house.
>
> MATTHEW 13:36

It is instructive that Jesus withdrew from the crowd (and the obligation I likely would have felt) to spend time with His disciples. The most important thing for Jesus was to pre-pare His disciples and not to "friend" several hundred people on an ancient FaceScroll. Clearly, it was valuable for Jesus to be teaching the crowds. But His relationship to His ministry "family" trumped the public gathering priority.

Jesus gave another example of schedule priorities:

> Immediately after this, Jesus insisted that his disciples get back into the boat and head across the lake to Bethsaida, while he sent the people home. After telling everyone good-bye, he went up into the hills by himself to pray.
>
> MARK 6:45-46

Jesus understood that He must say no to people who really wanted His attention in order to spend time doing what mattered most. This passage follows Jesus' miraculous feeding of five thousand people. If I had performed such a feat, I would have hung around for hours to soak up the praise and accolades, sign a few autographs, and take some selfies. But Jesus knew what He needed in that moment—time with His Father.

I need to know when to say no. Busyness does not define my worth. Being a schedule martyr does not make me more righteous. Overscheduling keeps me from spending time with the One who gives His righteousness to me.

Why does that happen time and time again to followers of Jesus? My personal belief is that one of the biggest and most damaging mistakes that the church makes with new believers is not teaching clearly and continually what happens when you put your faith in Jesus Christ as Savior and Lord. It seems that we too often get young Christians immediately into studies and activities, suggesting that change can happen only when you are trying hard and concentrating on the spiritual disciplines.

That was my struggle for forty years before I realized a simple truth. Dramatic change took place the moment I made that faith commitment to follow Jesus. Scripture tells me that when I decided to become a follower of Christ, the following things happened immediately:

I was given a new identity.
I became a new creation.
I received the gift of the righteousness of Christ.

I struggle with that concept because I am not always righteous in my behavior. That may well be the biggest understatement in this volume. Here is the amazing theology of the gospel: God sees me as righteous and worthy because of my relationship with Jesus. Nothing I have done or ever will do could earn that righteousness. It is a gift of grace because of the finished work of Jesus on the cross.

I was changed completely when I put my trust in Christ as my only hope for salvation. I did not have to struggle with futile performance to change. I was changed that day. But it has taken me forty years to know Him better, never realizing I had been carrying around the key to that kind of relationship since day one.

Now I see a different picture. I see Jesus standing at my side and explaining that I am completely changed. I see Him telling me that my sins are forgiven and I can quit relitigating past mistakes. I see Him explaining to me that all of those things that used to be true about me are no longer true. I see Him repeating that, because I tend to nod my head without really believing it. Jesus explains to me that no matter what the accuser might say, those things that used to define me are dead and buried at the Cross. I see Jesus telling me that I have the Holy Spirit to comfort me and provide an unshakable source of strength.

He reminds me gently that I don't have to grit my teeth and try harder to win favor and please Him. He tells me for the ten thousandth time that sin does not have power over me anymore. And I see His demeanor being just as patient and kind as the first time He told me that truth. I hear Him remind me that power over sin is looking to Him for my strength and not trying to fight it with my busyness and resolve.

I see Jesus looking deeply into my eyes and tenderly expressing (again) that it is my trust in God that pleases Him. No other works are required. My faith is what pleases Him according to God's Word. Nothing else. I picture Jesus embracing me and saying, "Relax. Rest. Let Me love you and then, out of that rest and love, you can love others. Quit making it so complicated, Dave."

I have a hard time putting my full weight on those truths.

But I have learned that we can disabuse ourselves today of the notion that busyness is somehow related to godliness. I suggest a spring (or summer/fall/winter) cleaning of the calendar. Allow yourself time to spend with the most important people in your life. Schedule time with Jesus. Don't allow guilt to monopolize every waking moment. Carve out time for friends, family, and yourself.

If Jesus could leave disappointed throngs behind for what was important, we should withdraw for recharging and time with God too. Write down where, when, and how you are going to find some time to relax with friends, family, and God. Be still, and know that God loves you and desires you. Your actions will naturally emerge from that loving relationship with Him. You don't have to earn that love. It is yours.

GOD'S TAKE

Be still, and know that I am God.

PSALM 46:10

A DOSE OF GRACE

Clean up your calendar by paring down your busyness. Limit or even eliminate activities, and create more time to be still with God and present with yourself and loved ones. What do you think can be readjusted to free up time for what's most important?

CHAPTER 4

THE ALL-IMPORTANT OWNER'S MANUAL

When all else fails, follow the instructions.

BUMPER STICKER

"Do not fold down the rear seats when occupants are in the rear seat area." This helpful bit of information actually appears on page 36 of the 2012 Nissan owner's manual.

I laughed at the absurdity of that warning when I read it, but then I thought maybe this actually happened to someone who got hurt or that it might just be lawyers proactively deciding to cover their rear seat area. That same owner's manual (which I may need to look for on eBay) warns owners not to "operate the key fob while on an airplane." *Who ever thought of doing that?* Mercedes Benz helpfully suggested in 2012 that the driver should "not switch off the ignition while driving," because some features would not work. You can't make this stuff up.

I have never read the owner's manual of any of the vehicles

I have owned—until something went wrong. I know that is highly offensive to my buddies who know everything about cars. But for some reason I never have the time or concentration to find out how my car can operate more efficiently and trouble free for a longer period of time. Why should I do that?

It is a woeful but, to be fair, often amusing pattern in my life. I don't read the instructions until I am in trouble. When I was assembling outdoor furniture for the summer, I attached the frame incorrectly to the glider, making it resemble a high-rider vehicle. Since I didn't think Joni would appreciate using a step stool every time she wanted to sit down, I decided to read the instructions and got it assembled correctly.

Our current rescued canine friend, Maggie, was an epic puller when she first joined our family. She is eighty pounds of four-wheel-drive power, and even at two-hundred-plus pounds, I had a hard time controlling her on our first few walks. Joni had no chance at all. It became apparent that we had to do something, or I would have had to have shirts tailored with one arm longer than the other. We found a harness called the Gentle Leader that I describe in my previous book as "amazing."[1] What I don't confess in that account is my first failed attempt with the harness. True to form, I only glanced at the instructions before attempting to put the harness on Maggie.

Somehow I managed to put the harness around her head with the ring for the leash clip sitting on top of her snout instead of below, where it should have been. Maggie gave me a look that spoke volumes. I swear I could hear her thinking, *I know I am only a dog who can't read, but this cannot possibly be right.*

Because I am me, I still tried to walk her. Maggie took

about twenty steps and then sprawled in the grass in protest. Her face said it all. *This is not going to happen.* I finally decided to read the instructions carefully and got the harness on correctly. What a difference it made! When I understood the proper procedure, the walks became fun for both of us.

My natural tendency to jump first and read the instructions later has a pretty serious application to my faith journey. If I believe the Bible, my instruction manual, is truly God's revelation to all of us, wouldn't it make sense that the Bible contains insight to operate more efficiently? Wouldn't it make sense to reference the instructions *before* I get into trouble?

The growing cultural trend is to dismiss or marginalize the Bible. People find something archaic or offensive in its pages to laugh or rant about, instead of investigating the truth claims of Scripture. Those who get up in arms by a single passage often dismiss much, if not all, of what the Bible proclaims. Author and pastor Tim Keller has an interesting take on our American tendency to be offended by anything that challenges our current lifestyle.

> In individualistic, Western societies, we read the Bible, and we have a problem with what it says about sex. But then we read what the Bible says about forgiveness—"forgive your enemy"; "forgive your brother seventy times seven"; "turn the other cheek"; "when your enemy asks for your shirt, give him your cloak as well"—and we say, "How wonderful!" It's because we are driven by a culture of guilt. But if you were to go to the Middle East, they would think that what the Bible has to say about sex is pretty good. (Actually, they might feel it's not strict enough!) But

when they would read what the Bible says about
forgiving your enemies, it would strike them as
absolutely crazy. It's because their culture is not an
individualistic society like ours. It's more of a shame
culture than a guilt culture.[2]

We are quick to find ways that unloving and graceless
misapplications of biblical texts have done harm, while dismissing the incredible positive impact this same book has
had on history. Commandments against murder, stealing,
and lying are the basis of our legal system. The teachings of
Jesus lived out by His early followers radically changed the
status of women and children. Biblical stories and charac-
ters flow throughout great literature and art. Much of the
true humanitarian work in medicine was born out of biblical conviction.

Keller goes on:

If the Bible really was the revelation of God, and
therefore it wasn't the product of any one culture,
wouldn't it contradict every culture at some point?
Therefore, if it's really from God, wouldn't it have
to offend your cultural sensibilities at some point?[3]

Yes, it should. If the Bible is the revelation of God, then it follows that this volume contains insights into my spiritual and
emotional DNA that only the Designer can fully explain.

An engineer can look at a design problem and provide a
solution. He or she designed the product and knows where
the problem exists and how the solution can be implemented.

A software designer can look into the code and find
the offending bug that wreaks havoc. The designer knows

how the program works. I believe that to be true about my design. God knows how my software is written and how to keep it virus free and functioning normally. I capitulate that "normal" may look a little different for me than it does for you, but that is my design.

Psalm 139 was part of the beginning premise of this book. In that text David writes about how we are formed. Keep in mind that he wrote about the miracle of conception and life centuries before sonograms and the advanced knowledge of DNA:

> You watched me as I was being formed in utter
> seclusion,
> as I was woven together in the dark of the womb.
> PSALM 139:15

Look at the language that David uses when he writes about how life is formed in the womb, using a word that the ESV translates as "intricately woven." The Hebrew word can be translated to *variegate*, which means to weave with multicolored threads. The word suggests the complex patterns and colors implemented by an embroiderer.

David could not have used a more apt illustration for the complex beginning of life than the handiwork of an embroiderer. I have seen one at work when Joni embroidered summer shirts for our grandchildren's recent beach trip. She designed cute matching crab designs on the front of the girls' shirts and lobsters for the boys. The process for each shirt involved more than thirty different steps, multiple thread changes, and other stuff that made my eyes glaze over. Even the process that Joni utilized is far too complex for me to consider.

Now consider our DNA. Elaborate, integrated threads

of information inscribe the strands of DNA that make us who we are. To say that something as finely balanced and complex as the human body is the result of sheer chance is incomprehensible to me. I know that opens me up to some intellectual scorn, but consider this.

According to Carl Sagan, a single human chromosome (a DNA molecule) contains 20 billion bits of information. But what does that mean? What if all this information were written in an ordinary book in contemporary language? Twenty billion bits are comparable to about 3 billion letters. If there are roughly 6 letters in the average word, the information contained in a single human chromosome is equivalent to about 500 million words. The average page of printed text contains approximately 300 words, which translates to roughly 2 million pages. Assuming the average book contains 500 or so pages, the information contained in a single human chromosome adds up to more than 4,000 volumes.[4]

Sagan goes on to conclude, "It is clear, then, that the sequence of rungs on our DNA ladders represents an enormous library of information. It is equally clear that so rich a library is required to specify as exquisitely constructed and intricately functioning an object as a human being."[5]

By the way, Carl Sagan was an astronomer and supposed atheist, and he believed this all happened by chance.

And yet that same information led former atheist Francis Collins to come to faith in Jesus as he studied the human genome.

As the director of the Human Genome Project,
I have led a consortium of scientists to read out the
3.1 billion letters of the human genome, our own
DNA instruction book. As a believer, I see DNA,

the information molecule of all living things, as God's language, and the elegance and complexity of our own bodies and the rest of nature as a reflection of God's plan.[6]

I have found that no volume addresses the most fundamental questions of humankind as completely as the Bible.

Why am I here?
Do I have a purpose?
Is there anything after death?
Is there a God?
Can I know God personally?
Is God a loving or vindictive force?
Why is there pain and suffering if God is loving?
How can I find happiness?

These questions are honestly examined in the Bible, through words and interactions in the stories of the people struggling with those same imponderables. People like you and me. The Bible does not sugarcoat the failings of the most revered biblical figures—it honestly explores evil, sin, consequences, suffering, and pain. It sets forth the basis for true justice for the poor and oppressed, something that people still seek today. I have found principles for success in marriage, parenting, work, leadership, and friendship. I see hope for the future when others say it looks bleak. I realize salvation requires nothing to be sacrificed, other than my unwillingness to confess my need.

This book holds a power unlike any other I have encountered. Do I struggle with some of it? Of course. But I can read a passage that I have read countless times before and, without warning, find my heart pierced by a truth that changes my current situation, if not my very life. I have discovered this verse to be completely true:

> The word of God is alive and powerful. It is sharper than the sharpest two-edged sword, cutting between soul and spirit, between joint and marrow. It exposes our innermost thoughts and desires.
> HEBREWS 4:12

For that to happen, I need to drop the defensiveness and allow the light of Scripture into the darkest recesses of my heart. That takes time and relationship.

Part of my own journey to reconnect with God and others, and disconnect from performance anxiety, is to intentionally spend daily contemplative time in the Bible. Being relaxed, not pressured to read one verse or five chapters. Digging out truths of theology or enjoying stories of flawed humans like me being used in God's grand purpose. Sitting down with the Bible, a cup of coffee, an open heart, and an attitude of expectation is remarkably filling.

I used to read with a performance goal in mind. *I need to read the Bible in a year. I need to finish this study.* Now I read with only the expectation that God will meet me there and direct our time together. That is one more step in waking up slowly to God and being present in the moment. Expecting grand revelations each time I read the Bible instead of warm fellowship with God is one more way I stub my toe on the sacred. God desires to slowly mold me in His timing as I spend time with Him. Relationships take time and presence.

I have always considered myself to be lesser than the learned theologians that surround me in Dallas, Texas, like ants at a picnic. Theologians are generally less annoying than the picnic intruders, but nonetheless intimidating. But the truth is that all of us are theologians to some degree. We all have a worldview that includes or does not include God.

The word *theology* comes from two Greek words: *theos*, meaning "God," and *logos*, meaning "word." So the precise definition is "a word about God." Every moment I spend in thoughtful meditation in God's Word, I am building my theology. Every concept that I wrestle with builds a worldview that informs and influences my daily responses. Every doubt I overcome or step I proceed in faith builds perseverance for the inevitable storms.

Comedian George Carlin put it succinctly. "I was thinking about how people seem to read the Bible a whole lot more as they get older; then it dawned on me—they're cramming for their final exam." That resonates with me, since my final exam date could soon be on the docket. That sentiment of cramming to try to measure up reflects my early church upbringing that the purpose of salvation is primarily to avoid hell. Since I discovered grace, my journey has been dramatically different. Now Scripture sharpens, softens, refines, redeems, corrects, inspires, and comforts me.

I suggest you sit down with Jesus and God's Word, not to study it or check off a daily task. This is about relationship. Reading a Gospel parable, a psalm, or an encouragement from the Word is simply hanging out with your Abba Father.

GOD'S TAKE

All Scripture is inspired by God and is useful to teach us what is true and to make us realize

what is wrong in our lives. It corrects us when we are wrong and teaches us to do what is right.

2 TIMOTHY 3:16

A DOSE OF GRACE

The Bible has become a cultural lightning rod for certain actions, instead of the inviting narrative it truly is. From Genesis to Revelation, the Bible is a love story where a heartbroken Father pursues His family, desiring each child to return to His bosom and care. The Bible offers amazing insight into our design, needs, and purpose. Find a translation that you enjoy reading, and quietly connect with God for a few minutes. Ask God through the Holy Spirit to meet you there, to reveal a thought or truth you can carry today.

CHAPTER 5

OPENING THE GIFT OF GRACE

When the mask of self-righteousness has been torn from us
and we stand stripped of all of our accustomed defenses,
we are candidates for God's generous grace.

ERWIN W. LUTZER

THE HILL COUNTRY OF TEXAS is a go-to place when Joni and I need space to decompress from life. The pace is slow. The people are laid back and friendly. The towns are the subject of country music lore. The late Waylon Jennings sang about kicking back in Luckenbach, Texas. Willie Nelson wrote about not worrying about worldly possessions because he always has his Hill Country home in San Antone.

We love the little town of Fredericksburg that was settled by German immigrants in 1846. The early settlers refused to learn English and spoke something called Texas German. There are a handful of elderly locals who still speak this fascinating hybrid language, and they might utter a phrase like *der cowboy* now and then. The local terrain features rolling hills that inspired the Hill Country moniker.

On one of our visits, beautiful vineyards and fields of spectacular wildflowers greeted us as we drove into town. We stayed at a little cabin away from Fredericksburg and drove country roads into town. Each day we passed a sheep pasture. On the first day, we chuckled about one adventurous sheep that had found a way to get through the fence and was now grazing happily in tall grass along the road. She seemed to know what she was doing, never getting too close to the dangerous highway. The next day she was there again, enjoying her freedom and a different grazing menu from the rest of the flock.

Then we spotted another sheep that had also tried to find greener grass on the other side of the enclosure. This poor creature had gotten stuck under the fence, and it had not taken long for the searing Texas heat to take her life. It was obvious that this unfortunate animal had everything she had needed on the safe side of the fence. She was clearly well fed. But the lure of something more enticing led her to danger. Oh, how God's creatures—which include us—are prone to wander and miss the blessings they already possess.

As a follower of Christ, I have everything I need to be content. Yet I wander, looking for something new or the latest trend in the church. What I was looking for in every book, program, study, and event was the sweet gospel of unconditional love, unmerited forgiveness, and complete acceptance. I was looking for grace. This line from poet Nancy Spiegelberg may be the most indicting summary of the grace I misunderstood for decades: "Lord, I crawled across the barrenness to You with my empty cup uncertain in asking any small drop of refreshment. If only I had known You better I'd have come running with a bucket."[1]

I am indeed awakening to the mystery, the majesty, and the unquenchable supply of grace given to me each moment.

Grace.

It is a word that has lost its power through misuse and overuse. Fearful grace objectors banter about the ridiculous concept of cheap grace as if I must be wary of receiving a gift from my Father in heaven. Are you kidding me? If I view grace like a sales pitch for a time-share resort, I am listening to the wrong voices. There are no strings attached with grace. No fine print. No hidden costs. No promises to lure me in that have not already and forever been fully delivered. Grace gives me full title to the resort and all the first-class amenities.

Grace.

Today I heard a radio commercial for those unfortunate folks (I have been there) who find themselves with too much credit card debt. The announcer made the astounding claim that you should not let the credit card companies tell you that you have to pay your debt—you may have to pay only a fraction of what you owe. My prideful heart immediately bowed up. What? I sacrificed and paid my debt, so why should these folks get off easy? And then it hit me. That was my problem with grace for so many years.

I want to pay my debt! I don't want charity. I don't need your help. I can work hard and pay off what I owe! But there is a problem with the sin debt. No matter how much I work, sacrifice, serve, give, study, fast, and pray, I cannot pay this debt. I can't even put a dent in it with my self-salvation strivings. Paul wrote that all of us fall short, and the distance between us and a holy God is irreconcilable. "Everyone has sinned; we all fall short of God's glorious standard" (Romans 3:23).

Everyone. Trying to make up the distance between my sin

and God's standard with my own good works is like trying to jump the Grand Canyon on a unicycle. It would seem almost comically impossible if the stakes were not so high.

So God comes along with a redemption plan so radical that we have a hard time believing it could be true. This is what I almost always hear when I share God's grace with unbelievers or fellow recovering legalists.

"Is this true?"

"Yes, it is," I affirm.

The follow-up question is the same one I asked when I first heard the grace message.

"Why haven't I heard this before?"

To be completely honest, I had heard versions of that message over my first few decades of faith. But my heart response to grace was like my response to the credit-card-debt avoiders. You have to do your part and earn your way.

Thank God I finally understood that I could not do it myself. I could not earn my way to righteousness. And more importantly, I finally understood that this was the best news ever. I could quit flailing and start trusting God's gift of grace.

You don't have to do anything but believe. Radical. Crazy. That is not the kind of plan that religious people would concoct, because there is no built-in control mechanism. Grace is wild and free and unpredictable. Religious people don't like that at all. So they call the wonderful news of God's gift "cheap." They say that having no work requirement will lead to abuse and even a license to sin.

To borrow from my brother Saint Paul, here is a trustworthy saying that deserves full acceptance: grace can never be viewed as a cheap gift. It cost Jesus everything. I challenge you to kneel at the foot of the cross and look up. There is nothing cheap about the transaction that Jesus suffered for you and me. Nothing causes me to lose my Sunday school lesson quicker than the cheap-grace posse. And yes, I know that some people misuse grace. There is a word for that.

Sin.

The truth is that grace is the only real antidote for sin and should never, ever, be the excuse for sin. Paul addressed the heresy that grace gives me license to sin, and he was rightfully dismayed (you might even say ticked off).

> Sin will have no mastery over you, because you are
> not under law but under grace. What then? Shall we
> sin because we are not under law but under grace?
> **Absolutely not!**
> ROMANS 6:14-15, NET (EMPHASIS ADDED)

Here is a sampling of other translations of Paul's undisguised chagrin expressed in Romans 6:15 at the very thought that the sweet grace of the gospel would be abused:

> God forbid! (KJV)
> Of course not! (NLT)
> May it never be! (NASB)
> By no means! (ESV)

If I were given the opportunity to communicate one message to every person in the world, it would be a no-brainer for me. I would beg every person to open his or her mind and heart to the outrageous grace gift that God offers freely to each one of us. And I'd do my best to convince the world that all you have to do is open that gift in faith. In fact, my final-act life verse is from the book of Acts.

> My life is worth nothing to me unless I use it for
> finishing the work assigned me by the Lord Jesus—
> the work of telling others the Good News about the
> wonderful grace of God.
>
> ACTS 20:24

I wish that everyone who hears the gospel message would comprehend the love that God demonstrates to everyone who will receive that love. Instead of turning His back on sinners who deserved just that, God chose to reach out to you and me with a radical plan for forgiveness. A plan that is unlike any other religion in history. Man-made religion *always demands something* to earn salvation. God's plan of redemption requires the lost to bring nothing to the table other than sin and need. Nothing. Any other presentation of the sweet gospel of Jesus Christ is a lie.

> God saved you by his grace when you believed. And you
> can't take credit for this; it is a gift from God. Salvation
> is not a reward for the good things we have done, so
> none of us can boast about it.
>
> EPHESIANS 2:8-9

Not a single requirement other than believing. A gift of grace. Grace that is so vast and inexhaustible that no sin or sinner can exceed the scope of this amazing grace to cover their sin and offer redemption. I coined an acronym for grace that only partially captures the immensity of God's love.

God's Radical And Complete Embrace.

God radically offers complete forgiveness and embraces me as His child. That is exactly the picture that Scripture paints in the story of the Prodigal Son. The son has rebelled, sinned, and suffered the horrible consequences of his actions. The son realizes his sin, and in humble desperation, decides to throw himself on the mercy of his father, believing he has lost all his privileges of being a son.

But nothing has changed for his father. It reads like a Hollywood story of tear-jerking redemption. A child who is lost and hopeless. A father who never quits believing in and loving his son. The son trudging toward an uncertain homecoming with eyes downcast. Hearing a commotion down the path that sounds like distant shouts of joy. Is it a party at the home that was once his? Then the sound of sandals pounding on dirt causes the lost son to look up. What he sees is one of the most remarkable grace stories in history.

> While he was still a long way off, his father saw him coming. Filled with love and compassion, he ran to his son, embraced him, and kissed him. His son said to him, "Father, I have sinned against both heaven and you, and I am no longer worthy of being called your son."
>
> But his father said to the servants, "Quick! Bring the finest robe in the house and put it on him. Get a ring for his finger and sandals for his feet. And kill the calf we have been fattening. We must celebrate with a feast, for this son of mine was dead and has now returned to life. He was lost, but now he is found."
> So the party began.
> LUKE 15:20-24

The father places the finest robe on his wayward son, most probably his own robe. The robe that was worn on the most special of occasions. The custom would have been for the son to bathe, don clean clothes, and then put on the robe. But in a stunning gesture of compassion, the father places his robe over his son's filthy garments. What a gift of unconditional acceptance. Brokenness and all hope of self-salvation stripped away. We all fall on grace when we are completely honest with our hearts.

The story is the same today. The Father ran to forgive me when I acknowledged my sin and need. While I was still dirty and clothed in filthy garments of sin, I was forgiven, accepted, justified, and wrapped in the robe of righteousness. I was no longer condemned. Satan would have me forget that the robe of righteousness is wrapped lovingly around me. The author of lies reminds me (constantly) that I still wear dirty clothing. He suggests that I don't deserve to wear the robe until I clean myself up. That is the power of this story. The robe of righteousness is never earned. It is a gift of grace. Even on my worst day the Father wraps me up in this precious garment because of His Son, Jesus.

How differently I would live if I remembered that truth every day. I am a saint. I am wrapped in the robe of righteousness. I am a new creature who is forgiven, accepted, and cloaked in this incomprehensible gift of grace. Even in my failure Jesus loves me anyway and just as much.

The more I understand the depth of grace, the more I am compelled to give grace generously and freely to a hurting world. If I am receiving grace, I must also give it. If I welcome the generous gift of grace, I must become more generous. If I accept the gift of forgiveness, I must forgive. If I marvel at God's unfailing love, I must also love others.

Today was one of those long days at work. I was tired. I am on deadline to finish the book that you are currently holding. I wanted to be left alone. And then God brought a hurting person into my path. Every part of me wanted to make an excuse and escape as she shared her trials. But I recognized her need, and I listened. I offered some encouragement and prayer.

My giving of grace when I would have preferred to do anything else made a difference for that wounded soul. I didn't do all that much except be available. That is exactly what I hope will happen when I inevitably need someone to share my sadness. That is how this grace thing works. That is what the doubting world is looking for from the church. Grace, forgiveness, and love.

As Jesus faced the horror of the Cross, He said to His disciples,

> Now I am giving you a new commandment: Love each other. Just as I have loved you, you should love each other. Your love for one another will prove to the world that you are my disciples.
>
> JOHN 13:34-35

Does my love prove that I am a follower of Jesus? Does my heart reveal that I comprehend the magnitude of His grace? Living out of grace is not a tiring burden. It is a joyous response of gratitude if we stay focused on the source of that grace.

But life happens.

Life gives me sadness, loss, and loneliness, but when I trust Jesus, I have hope in the darkest storm. It is hard to live in a community of grace. Legalism is so much easier than grace, because it allows me to assess someone's situation and apply a verse or assign a task. If that person rejects that biblical admonition or task, then legalism allows me to withdraw because he or she is disobedient. Grace does not give me that option. Grace demands that I move toward the struggle of my brother or sister and not away in judgment. No wonder grace is a tough sell!

Grace wears me out and lifts me up. Grace is frustrating and exhilarating. My old nature screams that people who make bad decisions over and over get what they "deserve." They don't "deserve" to be pursued and loved and restored. They made their bed—now let them lie in it. But there is a small, quiet voice in my heart that tells me that they have value. That they are loved by their Creator. And that voice asks: *Who are you to decide who "deserves" anything?*

Pastor Paul Donnan says it perfectly:

> Grace doesn't treat us better than we deserve. It treats us without the slightest reference to what we deserve. . . . Grace ceases to be grace if God withdraws it upon any human failure. . . . If Grace is in any way tied to something you do, then it is no longer a gift but a wage, and that's not grace.[2]

Would you open the outrageous gift of grace and accept it as a mind-blowing outpouring of love from a Father who delights in you? Whenever you feel sad, unworthy, stressed, angry, frustrated, or unloved, return to that open gift of inexhaustible grace. And bring a bucket this time.

GOD'S TAKE

God saved you by his grace when you
believed. And you can't take credit for
this; it is a gift from God. Salvation is
not a reward for the good things we have
done, so none of us can boast about it.

EPHESIANS 2:8-9

A DOSE OF GRACE

*Grace is by definition an undeserved gift. Look for
people in your life to whom you can give this gift
of acceptance, love, forgiveness, and kindness today.
Don't expect reciprocity when you give grace. This is
such an important piece to connect more with God
and others. Accept His grace as a wonderful gift,
and feel free to regift it over and over again.*

CHAPTER 6

NEW EYE
FOR AN OLD GUY

A baby is God's opinion that the world should go on.

CARL SANDBURG

Our family gathers at a Gulf Coast house every summer to enjoy the beach and one another. This past year I watched my four-year-old grandson, Ethan, run to the encroaching surf, turn, and run away over and over, with equal joy each time. He never seemed to tire of this game of tag with the advancing and retreating surf. His sweet mom, Holly, told us later that Ethan had perfectly summarized his love for the water.

"I love the ocean because it never stops playing."

The insight through the eyes of a child. How wonderful and sacred is their view.

I am now a few days into this attempt to disconnect from smartphones, busyness, and distraction, and I'm feeling convicted. Maybe part of the solution is looking at the world with the boundless curiosity of a child. Children's author Dr. Seuss described adults as "outdated children." Do we have to grow up that much? Can I still find delights in the daily routine? It requires altering the way I see my world. Even in the cacophony of the city I can delight in the sounds of birds chirping. I can be wowed by the aerial acrobatics of squirrels and be entertained by one of them taunting Maggie with chatter. Maggie was less than amused, running along the fence, as the agitating squirrel deftly leaped from the fence post onto our backyard elm tree.

I decided to do some investigation regarding squirrel speak. Squirrels use a combination of sounds and tail movements to communicate danger, emitting high-frequency calls for flying predators such as hawks. But that wasn't the sound I heard directed at Maggie, which was more of a barking sound, reserved for perceived land threats. In addition, squirrels have a variety of clucking sounds they use to communicate with each other. All this rodent talk had been happening right under my nose for years, but I never noticed. I discovered that these little critters can jump up to fifteen feet from tree to tree and can free-fall twenty feet and land softly on a branch. It's just one example of the complex and creative world that's already all around me, that I can see when I shift my eyes from a screen to my surroundings.

Recently Joni and I had a grandparents' day with our three-year-old grandbaby twins, Bennett and Clara, at an indoor playground. As we started to go inside, I realized I had left my phone at home. After the conditioned oh-no response, I relaxed and forgot about it. While the kids were playing, I was completely in the moment with them. When they pointed out something, I didn't look up briefly from the smartphone, nod, and smile. I actually watched and participated.

"Papa, watch me on the slide," Clara implored. Have you ever noticed how intently children watch your eyes to see if you are really paying attention? It is important. How sad that I have allowed e-mails and information to invade these sacred moments.

Bennett climbed to the top of the play structure. "Papa, look at me."

I could tell by their sweet smiles that they loved having "Papa" watch and approve of their every accomplishment. This is where my shame reflex kicks in. I have missed so many moments with them, even when I have been with them. I remind myself that a big part of my attempt to change my daily journey is not to dwell on past failures. I am looking to live today more connected to God and to others. If you share that regret reaction, I can empathize. But let's all understand that we are on this journey as partners to learn how to enjoy today more fully.

One of the greatest observers of children and how they view the world was cartoonist Bil Keane. His *Family Circus* comics captured those moments for decades. Keane wisely said, "Yesterday's the past, tomorrow's the future, but today is a gift. That's why it's called the present." I absolutely love that. Today is a gift that will happen just one time.

I was reminded of an earlier junket with all the grandkids to watch *Disney on Ice*, featuring all of the kiddos' favorites. There were ample opportunities for me to exercise my gift of cynicism during that event. Shameless promotion. Twelve-dollar popcorn. That is not a misprint. Twelve-dollar popcorn! One of the kiddos dropped a kernel, and I invoked my own five-second rule, because that was a dime's worth of corn!

But that night I merely smiled about the hawking of cheap souvenirs and the apparently diamond-dusted popcorn. I watched the event through the eyes of children who were enraptured in wide-eyed wonder at the magical spectacle. I watched Ethan's eyes light up when Jake and the Never Land Pirates sped around the ice. Clara was mesmerized by Elsa and Olaf. Bennett giggled in delight when Woody and Jessie joined in. Oh, to see the world with wonder like these innocent eyes did, without my adult filters of disappointment and cynicism. Remembering that night reinforces that one of my waking-up-slowly lessons is to get new lenses for my world-weary eyes.

Betty Smith framed the idea perfectly in *A Tree Grows in Brooklyn*. "Look at everything always as though you were seeing it either for the first or last time: Thus is your time on earth filled with glory."[1]

The eyes of a child. A child can find magic in the mundane. What happens to us when we start having to act like adults? I saw a T-shirt recently that said, "The worst decision I ever made was growing up." I concur.

I remember spending hours and hours as a child building Lincoln Logs forts. Once the fort was in place, I would meticulously line up little green soldiers ready for epic imaginary battles. During my aviation-obsession phase, I would fold paper airplanes in every different configuration I could conjure up to see which flew the straightest and farthest. I carefully logged the flight details to pinpoint the all-time perfect design.

Now my old-guy eyes see kids consumed by screens. But the truth is that kids haven't changed at all. Children have a wonderful curiosity for life. Have you noticed that a child can get bored with a toy in seconds, but they will play a simple, interactive game like peekaboo, hide-and-seek, or tag for as long as they have a willing playmate? There is a basic human-wiring message there—we are designed for human contact. And yet we allow them to become device-a-holics, following our examples.

To be sure, my mom used television as a way to distract me as a child. She needed to get things done now and then too. One of my leftover gifts from that time is that I can still flawlessly sing every word of the *Mister Ed* theme song. But there were inherent limits when I was growing up. There were no DVRs to play back recorded material. Children's shows were on in early morning and late afternoon. From midmorning until an hour before dinnertime, I had to find something to do.

I played Wiffle ball in the backyard with friends day after day and creatively adjusted the rules to fit the situation. For example, a ball hit into the garden of mean old Mr. Moore was an automatic out, because he would keep our precious game balls. I collected baseball cards and actually read the information on the back. Many cards were stained by the pink slab inserted in the packs that we were told by the card company was bubble gum. It tasted awful, but we chewed it nonetheless, because it was part of the baseball-card experience. The cards might have actually tasted better.

I remember catching sunfish on a simple fishing pole and finding tadpoles in a murky pond. I had a front-row seat for the nighttime light show presented by hundreds of lightning bugs on a sultry summer night. It was a simpler time to be sure, but the reality is that kids have not changed in their curiosity about the world since then.

There is an innate honesty with children. To your horror, children will repeat verbatim anything you shouldn't have said in the first place. My grandkids will tell me without hesitation when I have coffee breath. I remember having a conversation with my nephew Jon when he was a little boy. He had done something wrong, and I was discussing the implications of his behavior. He looked intently at me as I talked. I remember thinking what an impact I was having with my wise words. When I finished, little Jon asked me one question.

"Uncle Dave, why do you have hairs in your nose?"

Along with their uninhibited honesty, children often see the world with more moral clarity than we so-called "grown-ups" do. Jesus understood this gift that children possess, and He valued it more than the staid "wisdom" of the religious experts.

Jesus had some subversive teachings about children and women. We forget how revolutionary His message was in that culture. Children were viewed as expendable. In his book *When Children Became People: The Birth of Childhood in Early Christianity,* historian O. M. Bakke details Jesus' radical teaching among the people of His day. An infant boy was not named until the eighth day, and an infant girl was not named until the ninth day, enough time for parents to decide if they wanted to keep their child.[2] Those less fortunate infants, ones who were deformed or just happened to be girls, would often be killed or left to die of exposure.[3] Bakke makes a compelling case that civilization changed because of a radical rabbi's actions in moments like this from Mark's Gospel account:

> The people brought children to Jesus, hoping he might touch them. The disciples shooed them off.
>
> MARK 10:13, MSG

I always read this through modern eyes. The kids were just annoying the grown-ups. Go somewhere else and play!

But the real truth is that the adults believed those children had no right to be there.

> But Jesus was irate and let them know it.
>
> MARK 10:14, MSG

Some translations say Jesus was indignant. As a general rule, I would prefer that Jesus feels neither irate nor indignant toward me. I love the description, He *let them know it.* How many problems would be averted in the Christian community if we got angry about the right things and then talked with the people actually involved in those situations?

Here comes the good part—what Jesus said:

> "Don't push these children away. Don't ever get between them and me. These children are at the very center of life in the kingdom. Mark this: Unless you accept God's kingdom in the simplicity of a child, you'll never get in." Then, gathering the children up in his arms, he laid his hands of blessing on them.
>
> MARK 10:13-16, MSG

We can't comprehend how radical Jesus' words were to the people hearing them. This was a remarkable declaration of value. Children were truly disenfranchised in the Roman and pagan culture. Unwanted babies were left in public places as "unclaimed things," which could legally be claimed by whomever might want the child for whatever purpose. The child could become a slave, a play companion for another child, or a prostitute. Another could be mutilated, then sold for begging purposes. A Roman father could sell his son three times before he was declared free. Children were even treated as pets.[4]

Some children were loved and educated, but many, if not most, were kept simply for entertainment or gratification. This is uncomfortable to write about, but it helps to clarify how truly revolutionary the teaching of Jesus was and why the establishment hated Him so much. Jesus truly upset the "good old boy" system of both the pagan and religious cultures.

It is heartbreaking that our culture still does not take the words of Jesus seriously enough about the value of children and our responsibility to instruct them. To be sure, children are born with a sin nature. But they are also born without prejudice, bigotry, and classism. They are unimpressed by status and wealth. We adults teach them those things by our words, our lives, or our indifference.

In 1971, I was working as a local disc jockey in Ohio. The world was a scary place, and my generation was determined to make a difference. Our hearts were in the right place, but our strategy was flawed. We thought political change was the answer. I have since learned that changing the hearts of men and women is the answer, and that happens best through a relationship with Jesus.

One of the songs that impacted me deeply during my early DJ days was compiled by a Los Angeles disc jockey named Tom Clay. He remixed two hit songs from the sixties—"What the World Needs Now Is Love" and "Abraham, Martin and John," adding audio clips to create a compelling social commentary. The medley is as powerful today as when I listened to it as a young radio announcer.

The record begins with a child being interviewed about the meaning of segregation and bigotry, but the youngster clearly has no idea what those words mean.

Then Clay powerfully integrates excerpts of speeches by

John F. Kennedy, Robert F. Kennedy, Martin Luther King Jr., and Ted Kennedy's eulogy for his assassinated brother, Robert. Those moments are intercut with sound bites of news coverage of their tragic deaths and other news stories.

At the time, I didn't realize the implications of how volatile our country was during that period. My parents rarely shared their fears, but they must have wondered if my generation would have any hope at all with the violence and hatred running wild. Hearing those heart-wrenching sound bites mixed in with the lyrics from "Abraham, Martin and John" still makes me emotional.

"Abraham, Martin and John" laments that Abraham Lincoln, Martin Luther King Jr., and John and Robert Kennedy all died too young as victims of senseless hatred. As the lyrics ask if anyone has seen my good friend John, the remix interrupts with CBS broadcaster Walter Cronkite's special bulletin on November 22, 1963: President John F. Kennedy is dead.

The song turns to "my old friend Martin." Were King's words included in the song—"Difficult days ahead . . ."— a possible premonition of his own violent death? And when Senator Robert Kennedy pays tribute to Dr. King, lines from that speech are stitched into the lyrics, wondering who will be the next person to "suffer from some senseless act of bloodshed," an eerie self-prophecy. Kennedy would die during the presidential campaign of 1968.

The compilation gently transitions to the lyric "what the world needs now is love, sweet love," ending with the child's voice again, asked to define the word *prejudice*.

"Umm, I think it's when somebody's sick."

Spot on. Fast-forward fifty years, and it feels like not much has changed.

I am sick. So are you. Since the Garden of Eden all of us have been sick in our sin. Christians are forgiven, justified, and righteous because of Christ, but (and this is a big but) we are saints who still sin. We still have blind spots.

I don't know if those responses from the children in the song were spontaneous or scripted, but I do know that Jesus asked us to have the trusting heart of a child. Jesus is not saying that I should act childish and immature. If that were the case, I wouldn't need much teaching. Instead, he meant that I must have that childlike trust, dependence, surrender to authority, and need for relationship. A child isn't born hating another color, country, or idea. That is learned from adults.

Pray that God will allow you to see everyone you come in contact with today as a child sees him or her. Without prejudice or bigotry or judgment. That may prove harder than you expect. But that may reveal exactly how desperately you and I need new lenses.

GOD'S TAKE

About that time the disciples came to Jesus and asked, "Who is greatest in the Kingdom of Heaven?" Jesus called a little child to him and put the child among them. Then he said, "I tell you the truth, unless you turn from your sins and become like little children, you will never get into the Kingdom of Heaven. So anyone who becomes as humble as this little child is the greatest in the Kingdom of Heaven."

MATTHEW 18:1-4

A DOSE OF GRACE

Watch children at play and observe how they see the world. It could be revealed in something they do or say. Think about what you have lost from years of using adult "filters." Find delight in silly things and look for God in the everyday moments. Look for a moment in nature that reveals God's creativity. Look at other people without judging status or possessions. Just look in their faces and see the image of God. Pray that you will see something sacred with your new lenses.

CHAPTER 7

TIME TO RETHINK SABBATH

Most of the things we need to be most fully alive
never come in busyness. They grow in rest.

MARK BUCHANAN

God's sense of humor invades this project again. I began to rework this chapter on Sabbath and rest on a day when I got to sleep a little before sunrise. My television job with the Texas Rangers often involves traveling with the team after games. Most fans likely don't think much about the bizarre circadian rhythms of a baseball season. Last night's game finished just after 10 p.m. in Texas. One hour later, the buses left for the airport. Another hour to arrive, load up the plane, and depart. Subtract an hour traveling east. After a three-hour flight, more buses waited to take us to the hotel. I finally got to my room around 4 a.m.

This schedule is wearing even on the young and well-conditioned athletes who take the field. As fans, we have little concern about their schedule and how difficult it is to function at such a high level of athletic performance with erratic rest. We rationalize how much these athletes get paid and don't much care what obstacles the players face. But I get the difficulty of this life, and I respect the players immensely. Having said that, I need a nap.

No one gets the concept of rest better than my canine friend Maggie. She has a definite rhythm to her life.

Eat. Explore. Play. Sleep.

And then we repeat the cycle.

Maggie does not feel compelled to try to impress others. She explores until her curiosity is satisfied. And then she takes a guilt-free nap. Every day has rest moments for Maggie.

My life rhythm during a typical baseball season has historically not been conducive to physical and spiritual health.

Eat. Work. Browse. Try to sleep.

Devices have the ability to provide mindless distraction when I am tired. I am learning to untether and just let my mind relax, even if sleep is hard to come by. It is in quiet rest that I can recenter and regroup. Andy Crouch powerfully makes a case for the importance of this idea: "I rarely feel such clear signs of fatigue and anxiety on days that are filled with travel, meetings and assignments—only when I stop to rest. Without sabbath, I would be dangerously ignorant of the true condition of my soul."[1]

I believe it is time to rethink the concept of Sabbath. The word seems archaic and the concept unworkable in today's culture. But maybe we are missing another opportunity to discover sacred moments while we are stumbling over to-do lists, e-mails, and messages.

The idea of Sabbath is not an idea that humans would have conjured up on their own, especially the particular way that God defined it. Again, remember the cultural context this command was dropped into. It was a remarkable concept.

> No working on the Sabbath; keep it holy just as GOD, your God, commanded you. Work six days, doing everything you have to do, but the seventh day is a Sabbath, a Rest Day—no work: not you, your son, your daughter, your servant, your maid, your ox, your donkey (or any of your animals), and not even the foreigner visiting your town. That way your servants and maids will get the same rest as you. Don't ever forget that you were slaves in Egypt and GOD, your God, got you out of there in a powerful show of strength. That's why GOD, your God, commands you to observe the day of Sabbath rest.
>
> DEUTERONOMY 5:12-15, MSG

God makes it clear that all creatures, regardless of standing, need rest. Yet hundreds of years later, we still enslave ourselves to power, prestige, and possessions with little regard for the price we pay.

A remarkable article by Judith Shulevitz details how countercultural this commandment appeared to that society:

> The Israelite Sabbath institutionalized an astonishing, hitherto undreamed-of notion: that every single creature has the right to rest, not just the rich and the privileged. Covered under the Fourth Commandment are women, slaves, strangers and, improbably, animals. The verse in Deuteronomy that elaborates on this aspect of the Sabbath repeats, twice, that slaves were not to work, as if to drive

home what must have been very hard to understand
in the ancient world. The Jews were meant to
perceive the Sabbath not only as a way to honor
God but also as the central vehicle of their liberation
theology, a weekly reminder of their escape from
their servitude in Egypt.[2]

How sad that in today's world, declaring an intentional
day to do nothing is considered radical. But such a declaration of freedom from this nonstop culture is more important
than ever. In my lifetime we have made the term *after-hours* a
quaint anachronism of the past. Now I can go grocery shopping at 11 p.m. and then go work out at the twenty-four-
hour fitness center. I never need to worry about cash (if that
is still in use by the time you read this). I just go to the ATM
at the all-night convenience store.

When I was a youngster, the television stations actually
went off the air overnight and left nothing but a test pattern. Unless you were truly addicted to the glowing tube,
you had to find something else to do. Now my television has
more than seven hundred channels with around-the-clock
programming, and if that is not enough to occupy my time,
I can search on-demand shows.

I catch Maggie out of the corner of my eye, cycling again
from play to relaxation. After playing energetically for a few
minutes, she has crashed. She is indeed accomplished at this
concept of rest. The look of complete peace and satisfaction
on her face actually makes me a little jealous.

God modeled Sabbath rest at Creation. In Genesis we
read how God stopped, looked at His work, enjoyed it, and
then rested.

Then God looked over all he had made, and he saw that it was very good!

And evening passed and morning came, marking the sixth day.

So the creation of the heavens and the earth and everything in them was completed. On the seventh day God had finished his work of creation, so he rested from all his work. And God blessed the seventh day and declared it holy, because it was the day when he rested from all his work of creation.

GENESIS 1:31–2:3

God did not *need* to rest. He was modeling for His creation that *we* need to slow down and relax. Think of that. The God of Creation can kick back and enjoy what has been accomplished. Our Creator is telling us that we are creatures and not machines. What is wrong with us that we cannot take moments to enjoy and appreciate both our gifts of grace and the work of our hands?

The idea of Sabbath was a key distinctive of the early Puritan church in America. We "enlightened" modern believers often make fun of the strict customs of the early church leaders. We often use "puritanical" as a pejorative description of backward thinking. But the Puritans wisely understood that the body, mind, and spirit need rest and refueling time. Our culture has lost that instinct and ability to give ourselves permission to rest.

Jesus demonstrated that the command for Sabbath observance was not about following a hyperlegalistic rule. It was about taking the time to get over ourselves and see what God is doing. Remember this encounter with the Sabbath police?

One Sabbath, Jesus was strolling with his disciples through a field of ripe grain. Hungry, the disciples were pulling off the heads of grain and munching on them. Some Pharisees reported them to Jesus: "Your disciples are breaking the Sabbath rules!"

Jesus said, "Really? Didn't you ever read what David and his companions did when they were hungry, how they entered the sanctuary and ate fresh bread off the altar, bread that no one but priests were allowed to eat? And didn't you ever read in God's Law that priests carrying out their Temple duties break Sabbath rules all the time and it's not held against them?

"There is far more at stake here than religion. If you had any idea what this Scripture meant—'I prefer a flexible heart to an inflexible ritual'—you wouldn't be nitpicking like this. The Son of Man is no lackey to the Sabbath; he's in charge."

MATTHEW 12:1-8, MSG

While I am reasonably sure that Jesus did not say "lackey" to the Pharisees, it sure is fun to think about. But the point is that the heart of Sabbath is not rule keeping. It is resting in the One who is our Sabbath. I can acknowledge that God has this under control and He can get by just fine without my assistance for a few hours. Writer Wendell Berry captured the spirit of letting go of my need to control every moment: "Sabbath observance invites us to stop. It invites us to rest. It asks us to notice that while we rest the world continues without our help. It invites us to find delight in the world's beauty and abundance."[3]

The world gets along just fine without my help. That is disappointing and liberating at the same time.

Observing Sabbath is not as easy as just deciding to shut down one day. Perhaps that is why the religious leaders were so maddeningly intentional about what was allowed on that day. I think the original intent was to reinforce that resting requires a vigorous act of will. We almost always default to doing something. Religious people in our country tried to legislate Sabbath with the so-called blue laws on Sundays.

I remember rules about what you could and could not buy on Sundays when I was growing up. The only store open was Rexall Drugs. The store manager would rope off things you could not purchase on Sunday, and at times it seemed like a modern version of Leviticus. You could buy a screwdriver, but not screws. Brooms were banned for Sunday sales. You could not buy clothing with mixed fabrics. Oh, wait . . . that last one *was* Levitical. In my community, it wasn't a surprise that alcohol prohibition was a big deal.

The emphasis of the church on restrictions and not the inherent benefits of Sabbath predictably caused resentment. The beauty of Sabbath got lost in legalistic laws that communicated clearly that particular actions were more important than intentional rest and worship. We took the grace of Sabbath and made it about personal, man-made convictions.

The parallel of the difficulty of enjoying Sabbath and learning to be more present in this culture is intriguing. I am learning that this entire experiment of disconnecting from technology and busyness is surprisingly hard work.

It is hard, and there are seasons that make it harder. But the danger is that I say, "I'm going through a season," but then that season never ends. I may well manipulate God's plan for my well-being, but I will pay a price in burnout and compromised relationships.

Some of my fondest childhood memories were those

Sundays when my town was on retail "lockdown." We planned ahead for meals and visited friends and family. Now Sunday is just another "run errands and get stuff done" day. I am not advocating a return to blue laws. But it would be healthy to carve out an unplugged day for rest and relationships.

Noted author Dallas Willard, who possessed a far bigger brain than I have, says this about the fourth commandment: "The command is 'Do no work.' Just make space. Attend to what is around you. Learn that you don't have to *do* to *be*. Accept the grace of doing nothing. Stay with it until you stop jerking and squirming."[4]

Accept the grace of doing nothing. I love that thought. And I love the imagery of many of us jerking and squirming our way into Sabbath like fish out of water.

I failed to recognize how innocuous and mundane little activities add up, draining my life battery. For example, today I scheduled another lunch meeting. Said yes to another event. Agreed to another commitment. Each conversation, meeting, phone call, and commitment has a cumulative effect. I have a finite amount of physical, emotional, and spiritual energy. I must save some of that reserve for me, God, and those who matter to me most.

During my life I have typically exhausted my energy on people and things that I claimed were less important to me than my marriage, kids, and the Lord. That is why Sabbath is such an important concept. God says you need to accept this gift He has given, to take some time to recharge and be present with Him, your family, your friends, and even yourself.

Sabbath truly is vital to our very well-being. It can be a weekly oasis in the desert of busy living. God does not ordinarily clamor for my attention. He waits quietly for me to show up, be still, and spend time with Him. I don't do that often enough.

Let's enjoy the gift of Sabbath today. It's not just a good idea . . . it's the Law!

GOD'S TAKE

Jesus said to them, "The Sabbath was made to meet the needs of people, and not people to meet the requirements of the Sabbath."

MARK 2:27

A DOSE OF GRACE

Take a deep breath and mute the smartphone. Take a walk or sit in a favorite chair and listen to music. Believe that your value to your Father in heaven is unrelated to production. Your financial-portfolio worth might be related to working, but your eternal worth is not. Take the risk to rest in Him. Sabbath allows and encourages us to show up, so that God can meet us in those moments of rest.

CHAPTER 8

DON'T LET YOUR PAST STEAL YOUR PRESENT

*You can't start the next chapter of your life
if you keep re-reading your last one.*

MICHAEL McMILLAN

I AM ALWAYS INTRIGUED by Maggie's walk behaviors. For the most part she bounds from sniff to sniff, but I have noticed one interesting thing about her routine: she remembers certain things that happened on previous walks. For example, at the corner where we turn into our neighborhood, she always slows and looks intently into the bushes. A rabbit made its home there a couple of years ago, and Maggie encountered the bunnies a couple of times. Two years later, she still wonders if that might happen again. The creek is another spot where Maggie pauses, a place where she startled some mallards into flight. Or on our way home, we pass a particular house where a dog has often barked loudly, seeing us from the window or front door as we pass. Invariably, Maggie will stop and look at the house to see if he is there.

I have been reading a lot about how dogs think and how those thought processes order their responses. Some researchers think that dogs live in what they describe as an "eternal present." Maggie doesn't wake up thinking about being lost in North Texas like she was a few years ago—tired, scared, and hungry. She wakes up thinking about going out to sniff, doing her business transaction, and having breakfast. Nor does Maggie worry that tomorrow's breakfast may not be there. She doesn't fret that we may abandon her. She is more concerned about napping, chasing bugs, and the wonderful prospect of food.

I do not emulate this trait of my Labrador friend, but I am getting better. I used to spend a lot of time agonizing about the past. It can be just as dangerous to romanticize the past, thinking that life today is never going to be as good as it once was.

I love this E. L. Doctorow quote about writing: "It's like driving a car at night: you never see further than your headlights, but you can make the whole trip that way."[1]

That is profoundly simple and true. I think this principle applies to writing, living, *and especially for living a life of faith*.

Life is a fog. I wish I could see farther ahead on my journey, but the truth is, I cannot. I can see only as far as the light that illuminates my path. Because I'm a Christian, that is all I really need to know. Christ, my Light, reassures me that I can (and will) make the whole trip in that way. But there is fear in the unknown of the future, and it is easy to dwell in the predictable events of the past.

Not dwelling in the past is a huge issue to address on my journey to slow down, disconnect, and reconnect in healthier ways, both spiritually and relationally. I am learning a lot about what a mess I am. I am pretty sure most of those close to me were already aware of this.

Paul described his past to the church at Philippi. He wrote that what he used to view as valuable he now viewed as garbage, compared to the priceless value of knowing Christ. He explained his desire to know Christ better. And then Paul gave a note of encouragement and a path to achieve that goal by focusing on Christ and always moving forward.

> No, dear brothers and sisters, I have not achieved it, but I focus on this one thing: **Forgetting the past and looking forward to what lies ahead, I press on to reach the end of the race and receive the heavenly prize for which God, through Christ Jesus, is calling us.**
> PHILIPPIANS 3:13-14 (EMPHASIS ADDED)

That is the plan. I forget the past, look forward, and then take one stride at a time to the finish line. I can't backpedal and finish the race. I can't run in place and finish the race. I can't take one mighty leap to finish the race. I certainly can't stop and finish the race. It is about putting one foot in front of the other.

Forgetting the past is hard. I know that. I have struggled mightily, and at times quite unsuccessfully, with letting go of things that wounded me in the past. I remember being abandoned by a friend who was concerned more about his own self-interest than our long relationship. This person knew me and knew my heart. And yet in a moment of crisis, he questioned my motives and character, which was devastating. I fumed. I remember the feeling of betrayal and how painful that was to overcome. But time allowed me to step back and gain perspective. This person had been wounded in a similar situation. Fear won out when that scenario resurfaced with different people. I was able, with time, to forgive that moment.

Author John Claypool tells a wonderful story about his grandfather in Kentucky. A storm toppled a pear tree that had provided fruit for the family for generations.

> My grandfather was really grieved to lose the tree where he had climbed as a boy and whose fruit he had eaten all his life.
>
> A neighbor came by and said, "Doc, I'm really sorry to see your pear tree blown down."
>
> My grandfather said, "I'm sorry too; it was a real part of my past."
>
> The neighbor said, "What are you going to do?"
>
> My grandfather paused for a long moment and then said, "I'm going to pick the fruit and burn what's left."[2]

That is brilliant. The past is real. I can't pretend it didn't happen. I need to pick the good and even the rotten fruit to learn how it affected me. Then I burn what's left so I can heal and be present in the moment.

Maggie is a rescue pup, and we have no idea what happened to her prior to our adoption. She was found running loose in the country with a giant gash on her hind leg. She had worms and was malnourished. We don't know if she was wanted and lost, or abused and abandoned.

When we first brought her home, we had to be very careful when we opened doors and gates because Maggie was a "runner." She would take advantage of the slightest opening, and bolt. But here is the beauty of how Maggie and her canine counterparts function: after learning she could trust us, she relaxed.

Yesterday I went out in the front yard and didn't shut the

door completely. Joni noticed the door had swung open and went to close it.

"Dave," she called.

I turned around.

"Look," she said, while pointing down at Maggie.

Maggie knows she is not supposed to run out the front door, so she was lying down on the doorsill with two paws in the promised land. She was quivering with anticipation and fervent hope that I would give her the word to come on out. What a change from our puppy that would have been high-tailing it through the neighborhood just a couple of years earlier. Now she isn't looking to dash away whenever she gets a chance. The past is forgotten. What Maggie knows is that she is safe for this moment. She wants to be with us. With a hearty amount of praise, I quickly gave her permission to come join me outside.

Isn't that a lesson for us? I also have things in the past that have hurt me or frightened me. When I face similar situations, I am tempted to run or hide. Because of Christ, I know that I will not be abandoned or unloved. Every day that I wake up and focus on my Protector, Jesus, I know that I can relax and live in the moment. Some days I can live with joy. Other days are not so joyful, but I can always live in the assurance of the heavenly prize for which God, through Christ Jesus, is calling us.

Satan wants desperately to have me wallow in regret or shame of the past. Followers of Christ have an escape plan. It's not always easy to implement. Sometimes professional counseling is needed to break the chains. But the power for healing is there. Bible teacher and author Warren Wiersbe offers a good perspective on this challenge, as he analyzes how Paul related to the past.

"Forgetting those things which are behind" does not suggest an impossible feat of mental and psychological gymnastics by which we try to erase the sins and mistakes of the past. It simply means that we break the power of the past by living for the future. We cannot change the past, but we can change the *meaning* of the past. There were things in Paul's past that could have been weights to hold him back (1 Tim. 1:12-17), but they became inspirations to speed him ahead. The events did not change, but his understanding of them changed.[3]

I can't magically erase the events and pain of prior events, but I can break their power. *I can change the meaning of the past.* I can live for the future. I can believe that I am a new creation because of the finished work of Christ. And I can begin to see myself as God sees me. God knows all of that bad stuff about me, but He chooses not to remember any of it. When the Accuser tries to convict me of those events, his indictments fall on deaf ears. The past does not define me; Jesus does. Prior events and hurts do not defeat me, because I can advance, one step at a time, toward the goal set before me.

One of my favorite Olympic memories involves a runner who was the last to cross the finish line. Derek Redmond was an elite athlete who had a chance to bring home a medal in 1992 as Great Britain's 400-meter representative. After an injury-plagued career, Redmond seemed ready to leave a lasting legacy at the Barcelona Games. He had recorded the fastest time in the first heat and won his quarter-final race.

Redmond started well in the semifinal, but about 150 meters into the race his hamstring snapped, and he collapsed in agony. Medical personnel rushed to his aid, but Redmond waved them off. He struggled to his feet and began to hobble around the track. He was going to finish the race.

Cheers rang out for the actual winner of the race, but then the crowd of sixty-five thousand in the stadium began to comprehend the drama unfolding of a solitary figure limping in agony toward the finish. The spectators rose as one to encourage the courageous athlete. Another official offered help and was brushed away. Suddenly, a man broke through security and ran onto the track.

It was Derek Redmond's father. Derek heard a familiar voice and recognized this helper. He buried his face in his father's chest and sobbed.

Jim Redmond told his son that he was loved and didn't have to do this. But Derek set his eyes toward the finish and simply said, "Yes, I do."

His father replied, "Then we will finish this together."

Leaning on his father's shoulder, Derek Redmond limped to the finish line. Near the end Jim let his son go so he could cross the finish line on his own. A standing ovation greeted Redmond. The Olympic records state that Derek Redmond did not finish, because he received help. I would argue that no Olympian has ever finished better than Derek Redmond. He refused to let adversity keep him from the prize of finishing the race. Not winning. *Finishing.* That is such a beautiful image of how our earthly race often looks. I suspect that many who achieve heavenly standing ovations will finish with a limp and with eyes focused solely on Jesus.

That is how I see my race that Paul describes so beautifully.

Forgetting the past and looking forward to what lies ahead, I press on to reach the end of the race and receive

the heavenly prize for which God, through Christ Jesus,
is calling us.

PHILIPPIANS 3:13-14

When I fall or am hurt again, I know that I can bury
my face in the comforting chest of Abba Father and *we will*
finish together.

GOD'S TAKE

**This means that anyone who belongs to
Christ has become a new person. The old
life is gone; a new life has begun!**

2 CORINTHIANS 5:17

A DOSE OF GRACE

*The events of the past cannot be ignored. But we
can change the meaning of the past, because we
have a new identity. Write down those hurts that
keep you from looking forward to what lies ahead.
What injuries are keeping you from running well?
Determine what you can learn from the good and
bad fruit of those hurts, and then pray for the
strength to burn the rest.*

CHAPTER 9

BEGRUDGINGLY

To carry a grudge is like being stung to death by one bee.

WILLIAM H. WALTON

MAGGIE IS A WORK IN PROGRESS. She arrived with the baggage that rescued puppies often carry, and we have been ever so slowly unpacking those unknown bags. We have made great progress, and she is a truly sweet soul. But one maddening behavior still surfaces on occasion.

Selective hearing.

Maggie can hear a fly buzz across the yard, but somehow can't "hear" her name at eighty decibels from five feet away. She will just lie there unresponsive, without initiating eye contact. She subscribes to the common canine theory that "if I don't make eye contact, they can't see me." I know that I need to be consistent in my approach to this behavior, but sometimes I get impatient and simply up the decibel ante.

"Maggie!"

She stirs slightly to let me know she is still conscious.

"Maggie!!!"

Finally she gets up slowly, ambles toward me, stops, stretches lazily, and then comes to me begrudgingly.

That trait of my canine buddy came to mind as I considered another attitude I have that can disconnect me from God and others. It is my tendency to let go of anger or bad feelings toward others begrudgingly—if at all.

I picture the quiet voice of the Spirit seeking my attention. "Dave."

I am unresponsive because I don't want to give up my grudge. God can see me, but He doesn't yell at me to get my attention and force my obedience.

One particular face comes to mind as I write these words. This person damaged my relationship with one of my television clients. After hearing what he had done, I held an enormous grudge, even though God more than took care of me with other work. Seeing that person would cause my pulse to quicken. I carried that grudge for way too long, until I finally allowed God to get my attention.

"Dave, let it go. I have you in My hand."

Thankfully, the visceral response I once had to this person is gone.

Let's be honest. Sometimes it can be a fun exercise to hold a grudge. The other day I saw a person wearing a T-shirt that said, "Life is too short to hold a grudge. Slash some tires and call it even," and I made a mental note not to offend him.

That kind of revenge can be oh so tempting. But honestly, that attitude is unhealthy and counterproductive to our spiritual and emotional well-being. Paul's call for unity is just as needed today as it was in Ephesus millennia ago.

"Don't sin by letting anger control you." Don't let the sun go down while you are still angry, for anger gives a foothold to the devil.

If you are a thief, quit stealing. Instead, use your hands for good hard work, and then give generously to others in need. Don't use foul or abusive language. Let everything you say be good and helpful, so that your words will be an encouragement to those who hear them.

And do not bring sorrow to God's Holy Spirit by the way you live. Remember, he has identified you as his own, guaranteeing that you will be saved on the day of redemption.

Get rid of all bitterness, rage, anger, harsh words, and slander, as well as all types of evil behavior. Instead, be kind to each other, tenderhearted, forgiving one another, just as God through Christ has forgiven you.

EPHESIANS 4:26-32 (EMPHASIS ADDED)

After reading that passage, it's hard to make a case that holding a grudge is okay. The very last thing I want to do is bring sorrow to the Holy Spirit by the way I live.

I remember obsessing with Joni over that work situation I described earlier, and I used the phrase that I felt "weighed down." I had no idea that feeling might have been physically true. An article at *Science of Us* reported that researchers at Erasmus University found that carrying a grudge can *literally* weigh you down. According to a new paper published in *Social Psychological and Personality Science*, 160 undergraduates were recruited to participate in two supposedly unrelated experiments. The first exercise asked some students to write about a time when they suffered harm but forgave the other party. The second group were told to think about a similarly painful situation in which they didn't forgive the offender. A third group, which was the control, wrote about a normal social interaction like a normal conversation with a coworker that did not involve forgiveness.

They were then given a small physical challenge: jumping five times, as high as they could, without bending their knees.

After controlling for such factors as overall fitness and regular amounts of physical activity, the researchers found those who had written about forgiveness jumped higher, on average, than those who had just recalled incidents marked by a lack of forgiveness. Melissa Dahl summarizes: "Those who had been thinking about a time when they'd forgiven jumped highest, about 11.8 inches on average; those who had written about their grudges, on the other hand, jumped 8.5 inches—a huge difference, and a startling illustration of how forgiveness can actually unburden you."[1]

Dahl comments, "In a similar experiment reported in the paper, people who'd been prompted to think about a time they held a grudge estimated that a hill was steeper than people who were thinking about a time they forgave someone. The results suggest that the 'weight' of carrying a grudge may be more than just a metaphor."[2]

The lead researcher for the study writes, "A state of unforgiveness is like carrying a heavy burden—a burden that victims bring with them when they navigate the physical world. Forgiveness can 'lighten' this burden."[3]

Sometimes I can't even recognize the weight of something I've been carrying. It is only when I experience the freedom of its release that I understand how much that burden has weighed me down.

I wasn't at all surprised that our Creator often commented on this very human tendency:

> **Do not** seek revenge or **bear a grudge** against a fellow Israelite, but love your neighbor as yourself. I am the LORD.
>
> LEVITICUS 19:18 (EMPHASIS ADDED)

And Paul offers a friendly reminder to some first-century believers:

> I urge Euodia and Syntyche to iron out their differences and make up. **God doesn't want his children holding grudges.**
>
> PHILIPPIANS 4:2, MSG (EMPHASIS ADDED)

I think we can all agree that God is not honored when we hold grudges, especially against fellow believers. I can disagree with you, but unless the issue is heresy, I do not have permission to dismiss you. We need to iron it out and make up.

That is not the easiest path. My default response when I am wronged is usually sinful, and I take a little comfort that I am not unique. A couple of guys who were really close to Jesus had the same sinful response to bad behavior:

> He sent messengers ahead to a Samaritan village to prepare for his arrival. But the people of the village did not welcome Jesus because he was on his way to Jerusalem. When James and John saw this, they said to Jesus, "Lord, should we call down fire from heaven to burn them up?"
>
> LUKE 9:52-54

My response? You betcha! Fire! Bring it, Jesus! But what was His response?

> Jesus turned and rebuked them. So they went on to
> another village.
> LUKE 9:55-56

As much as my heart cries out for vindication and revenge, Jesus says no. You go on to the next village. You trust God. You forgive. This journey is hard because my sense of justice says that maybe they deserve fire from heaven.

But it gets even tougher. Jesus says to forgive my enemies.

I resist with my well-rehearsed five-step program. Step one is to blame someone else. Step two is to vow not to back down and give in because, after all, I was wronged. Step three is to go into hiding and despair. Step four is to be too proud to lose the battle. Step five is to hang on to the grudge, even as the weight of that animosity crushes my spirit.

That is an ugly little sequence, but it is a pattern I have repeated far too many times in my journey. I imagine Jesus' heart is saddened by my stubborn refusal to consider His forgiveness extended to me and, consequently, my refusal to lean on His power to forgive.

There is fear on that road to forgiveness, when I take my eyes off of Christ. My heart cries out in protest. What if they reject, scoff, or take advantage of my forgiveness? Jesus reminds me gently that He understands. And it is the right thing to do, no matter how the other party responds. Sometimes truth is irritating.

When I break those chains and allow God to heal my heart, the weight of the world is lifted off my soul. Sadly, too often, it is the road less taken. But it is the path that will make a difference in my (and your) journey with Jesus.

I love these principles of Christian living, often attributed to St. Augustine: "In essentials, Unity. In non-essentials, Liberty. In everything, Love."

What would the impact of the gospel be if the body of Christ lived by that simple little credo? Satan knows all too well how a world that is shown God's real love and grace would respond. So the enemy reminds me of grudges both real and enhanced. I turn from forgiveness because I convince myself that my offender does not deserve it. I conveniently forget that I did not deserve forgiveness either. There is no way I have found to release those grudges without the healing power of forgiveness. Author Will Davis Jr. explains:

> Once you decide to forgive, you initiate the healing process. Forgiveness gives your soul permission to move on to the higher and healthier ground of emotional recovery. Forgiveness is to your soul what antibiotics are to infection. It is the curative agent that will help to fully restore your soul. It doesn't immediately remove the pain of the offense but it does start you on the road to recovery.[4]

I really like that perspective. The decision to forgive initiates but does not complete healing. You and I will, in time, heal. But we will never get there without taking the first step of faith. Would you decide to lighten your load today?

GOD'S TAKE

When you assume the posture of prayer, remember that it's not all *asking*. If you have anything against someone, *forgive*—only then

will your heavenly Father be inclined
to also wipe your slate clean of sins.

MARK 11:25, MSG

A DOSE OF GRACE

*Trust God to balance the scales of justice. Giving
your grudges over to Him is freeing and will allow
you to initiate the healing process. Prayerfully ask
God to begin the healing process of forgiveness in
you, knowing that only time and God's mercy can
fully heal. As you start down that road to forgiveness and empowerment, discard the grudges that are
weighing you down. You won't get there today or
tomorrow, but it will happen. Life really is too short
to carry grudges!*

CHAPTER 10

GRATITUDE RHYMES WITH ATTITUDE

Gratitude turns what we have into enough.

MELODY BEATTIE

WE ARE NEARING THE HALFWAY MARK of this experiment to quit going steady with my device and just be friends. I think that analogy works for my bride, who has often registered frustration with my fawning over the phone and maybe, on rare occasions, not being completely present with her. (Joni will not be taking any questions on that last comment.) At any rate, this exercise has caused me to notice things that once passed me by, and the lessons are helpful.

Today I stopped during a road trip for the usual infusion of a caffeinated product. I visited the coffee shop restroom first and noticed that it could use a bit of attention. But I recognized that this was an extremely high-volume pit stop and gave the workers some grace that they were trying to keep up with drink orders more complex than the tax code.

An article on *Quora* named the most complicated Starbucks

order of all time: a Venti, half whole-milk, one-quarter one-percent, one-quarter non-fat, extra-hot, split-quad-shots (1½ shots decaf, 2½ shots regular), no-foam latte, with whip, two packets of Splenda, one Sugar in the Raw, a touch of vanilla syrup, and three short sprinkles of cinnamon.

If I worked the counter and heard that order, I would curl up on the floor in the fetal position and whimper quietly until help arrived. But God raises up people who can handle that kind of stress. I try not to be high maintenance, so I order my Grande Americano and leave quietly.

As I was waiting for my drink to arrive, a woman rejoined her husband after visiting the aforementioned restroom. She left no doubt about her feelings.

"I have never seen such a disgusting and filthy mess. There were paper towels overflowing the containers."

Her face looked like she had just left a construction-site portable toilet on a searing summer afternoon. Seriously? You have never seen such a disgusting mess? A few paper towels on the floor drives you to that level of hyperbole? Have you seen the conditions that people live in around the world? Do you see the conditions the poor endure in our own country? This coffee shop restroom is distressing you that much?

I was reveling in self-righteous judgment, and then it hit me. That is me. I complain about minor aggravations as if they were *actual problems*. And yet my first response was to condemn this woman. This "renewing of the mind" stuff is convicting and not much fun.

I thought about how much I dislike being around people who find fault with everything and, conversely, find little to be grateful for. I know that I look for any excuse to remove myself from their company. But until I came across the following study, I had no idea how important it was to avoid ingrates.

Neuroscientists have learned to measure brain activity when faced with various stimuli, including being involved in a full-on gripe fest. The results are sobering: "Being exposed to too much complaining can actually make you dumb. Research shows that exposure to 30 minutes or more of negativity—including viewing such material on TV—actually peels away neurons in the brain's hippocampus."[1]

The hippocampus is the part of the brain involved in problem solving. So scientists have determined that complaining or listening to complainers makes us less able to solve problems. This is not a risk I can afford to take. The article offers some ideas on how to keep your neurons safely in place, but I decided to go back to the Owner's Manual.

James reminds us that all gifts come from God:

Whatever is good and perfect is a gift coming down to us from God our Father, who created all the lights in the heavens.

JAMES 1:17

Paul pens a pretty strong directive:

Be thankful in all circumstances, for this is God's will for you who belong to Christ Jesus.

1 THESSALONIANS 5:18

I get it. I should be thankful for both clean and not-so-clean restrooms. I don't mean to be flippant, but the point is that being grateful really is an attitude. Gratitude is a mindset, and I am praying that the response of appreciation can become a lifestyle for me, with some practice.

It is easy to be grateful for the good things. Accepting

with thankfulness the bad and sorrowful takes faith and trust that God is faithful with His children. I cannot claim to be grateful until I can simply say thank you for everything that comes my way, recognizing that every event will bring joy, character, perseverance, or ultimately, glory to God.

Roman philosopher Cicero wrote that "gratitude is not only the greatest of virtues, but the parent of all the others." Hmmm. I can see how that plays out. I forgive others out of gratitude for my own forgiveness. I give grace because I am grateful I was offered grace when I did not merit that gift. I give to those less fortunate out of gratitude for my financial blessings. Cicero might have been on to something.

The psalmist knew the power of giving thanks for the blessings of life.

> On your feet now—applaud GOD!
>   Bring a gift of laughter,
>   sing yourselves into his presence.
>
> Know this: GOD is God, and God, GOD.
>   He made us; we didn't make him.
>   We're his people, his well-tended sheep.
>
> **Enter with the password: "Thank you!"**
>   Make yourselves at home, talking praise.
>   Thank him. Worship him.
>
> For GOD is sheer beauty,
>   all-generous in love,
>   loyal always and ever.

PSALM 100:1-5, MSG (EMPHASIS ADDED)

I got a chuckle thinking about having to log in to access God in prayer. Using the password "thank you" would be a pretty good way to prepare my heart, and a reminder every time to appreciate all of my blessings.

Perhaps the following story is a bit indelicate, but it always makes me smile. President Ronald Reagan had a favorite joke he told so often that the joke itself became a joke with staff members.

The joke concerns twin boys of five or six. Worried that the boys had developed extreme personalities— one was a total pessimist, the other a total optimist—their parents took them to a psychiatrist.

First the psychiatrist treated the pessimist. Trying to brighten his outlook, the psychiatrist took him to a room piled to the ceiling with brand-new toys. But instead of yelping with delight, the little boy burst into tears. "What's the matter?" the psychiatrist asked, baffled. "Don't you want to play with any of the toys?" "Yes," the little boy bawled, "but if I did I'd only break them."

Next the psychiatrist treated the optimist. Trying to dampen his outlook, the psychiatrist took him to a room piled to the ceiling with horse manure. But instead of wrinkling his nose in disgust, the optimist emitted just the yelp of delight the psychiatrist had been hoping to hear from his brother, the pessimist. Then he clambered to the top of the pile, dropped to his knees, and began gleefully digging out scoop after scoop with his bare hands. "What do you think you're doing?" the psychiatrist asked, just as baffled by the optimist as he had been by the pessimist.

"With all this manure," the little boy replied,
beaming, "there must be a pony in here somewhere!"[2]

I know that some seasons of life are difficult, and some
days you just hope to survive. But I think that the majority
of us would admit that we can find something to be grateful
for, even in moments of frustration.

Gratitude is the stabilizer for my spiritual walk. I think
I can make a pretty good case that growing a grateful heart
is the foundational attitude of the fruit of the Spirit—love,
joy, peace, patience, kindness, goodness, faithfulness, gentleness, and self-control. It is that important. Gratitude keeps
me from envy, if I can mentally pivot to the many things
I am blessed to enjoy. Gratitude keeps me from anger, if I
can be grateful for how patient God is with my myriad of
shortcomings. Gratitude keeps me from frustration, when it
reminds me how much worse things could be.

I have programmed a trigger into my gratitude response.
When I start getting cranky about my back pain, I think
of my friend Mike (and others) who live in constant pain.
I become grateful that my pain is not constant, and I am
reminded to pray for them. A simple mind-set change can
take me from self-pity to prayer for others.

I am also being prompted to pray for anyone who makes
me angry with his or her thoughtlessness or rudeness. What
is hurting that person's heart so much that the response is
filled with such venom? Full disclosure . . . I am not there
yet. But when I can respond with an attitude of gratitude, it
is the most freeing feeling. Maybe that is the best way to be
grateful consistently. When I get outside my little world and
see the suffering and sadness around me, I fall to my knees
in thanksgiving for how fortunate I am.

Today when you find yourself being tempted to complain, pray for a grateful heart, and see if you see a pony in there somewhere. There almost always is.

GOD'S TAKE

Do everything without complaining and arguing, so that no one can criticize you. Live clean, innocent lives as children of God, shining like bright lights in a world full of crooked and perverse people.

PHILIPPIANS 2:14-15

A DOSE OF GRACE

Look for something to be grateful for today and every day. Especially think of something you are grateful for when circumstances don't warrant that response. When a driver cuts you off in traffic, be grateful you are safe. When you are getting slow service at a restaurant, be grateful you have money to buy food. Pray for the people who irk you, asking God to help them with whatever sadness, hurt, or pain is causing their responses. Share your feelings of gratitude with God and others.

CHAPTER 11

WORRYING
STEALS THE MOMENT

Don't worry about the world coming to an end today.
It is already tomorrow in Australia.

CHARLES M. SCHULZ

It was nap time at our house for twin grandkids Bennett and Clara. But things were not going smoothly in persuading Bennett to go to his normal upstairs bed. Earlier, sweet Bennett had a bad dream about a pig residing under his bed, and he was having no part of that bedroom today. I knew that young children tend to worry about animals, imaginary creatures, and the proverbial monster under the bed. So instead of dismissing his concern as silly, we addressed the situation. We had to make that room pig free!

I assured Bennett that our Labrador friend Maggie was a skilled and dedicated pig hunter. Together, Maggie and I marched upstairs for Operation Safe Sleep, on a mission to secure the area from all porcine threats. After an appropriate amount of time, we returned and reported that the pig was gone.

Bennett accepted our mission report and was able to sleep. Bennett still talks about the pig that once lurked under his bed. We adults smile about such a silly concern. But for him it was a real and present concern. And if we are honest, our worries are often just as unlikely as Bennett's concern about a pig under the bed.

I am the son of a worrier. I loved my dad, and I learned so much from him that I have tried to emulate as a leader and father. But there was one of his traits I have not tried to adopt: his propensity to worry.

I used to fly constantly for my job. If there was a plane crash or incident anywhere in the civilized world, I would expect a phone call.

Ring.

Me: "Hello?"

Dad: "You're okay! Just wanted to make sure."

You might know from geography class that Texas is a really big state. So we have lots of weather incidents. A tornado could happen nine hours away from our home and still be within the Lone Star State.

Ring.

Me: "Hello?"

Dad: "You okay?"

Me: "Yeah, Dad. That storm was in El Paso. That's more than six hundred miles from us."

Dad: "Just wanted to make sure."

It still makes me smile to think about how much he cared, but I learned from watching my dad's excessive worrying that a lot of what we worry about is not worth the time. Worrying steals the moment, although I will concede that some things are worth worrying about, such as the following:

If your car horn sticks and won't stop as you follow a group of Hell's Angels. *That might be concerning.*
If your refund check from the IRS bounces. *Worth some angst.*
If the bird staring in your window is a vulture. *Maybe that should give you pause.*

I heard a story about a patient running down a hospital corridor toward the elevator just minutes before his scheduled surgery.

A receptionist stopped him with this question: "Where are you going?"

The patient answered, "I heard my nurse say, 'Don't worry. It is a very simple operation, and I'm sure it will be okay.'"

The receptionist replied, "Why does that worry you? She was just trying to comfort you."

"She wasn't talking to me," the patient responded. "She was talking to my doctor!"

Albert Einstein offered this interesting theory (one I can actually understand). "Women always worry about things that men forget; men always worry about things women remember." If you didn't think Albert Einstein was a genius before, that quote reveals the depth of his intellect. After all, Joni spends a fair percentage of her time wondering what important thing I have forgotten to do. I spend a fair amount of my time worrying about what Joni is going to ask me that I have totally forgotten to do.

The truth is that most things don't merit the energy of worrying.

The premise of this journey we are on together is simple. We are the most connected culture in history. But we are the most disconnected from God and one another. So far I have tried to wean myself from my ever-demanding devices, recognize that busyness is not necessarily a merit badge, and see that rest is a command from our Creator.

I have explored the insight into my design as detailed in the Bible, and the power of receiving the gift of grace. I have considered looking through the untainted eyes of a child and not dwelling in the past. I am working on giving up my too-often cherished grudges and finding something to be grateful for every day.

Some of these grace suggestions have been building blocks to creating intimacy with God, the relational steps that allow me to experience His love and care. Other grace suggestions have sought to limit impediments to my connection to God and others. These are attitudes that keep me from being able to focus on God. Worry is near the top of the list for many folks.

"Worry is like a rocking chair. It gives you something to do, but it doesn't get you anywhere." That old proverb came to mind as I read a study about the link between increased worry and the risk of stroke. After adjusting for other behaviors, researchers discovered that participants with the highest level of anxiety factors had a 33 percent higher risk of stroke than those in the lowest range of anxiety.

The study was sobering on a personal level. My dad died from complications of a stroke. Worry steals joy and peace from its victims. I saw it with my dad, and I see it all around me.

As I get older, I experience more and more how practical Scripture is for daily living. In the teaching of my youth, the Bible was a book of lofty and seemingly impossible demands to behave in a way that would please God. Now I see that the Bible is a love story where Jesus met those impossible demands on my behalf. I see now that my simple faith and trust pleases God. And I see a practical book that shows me how to find joy during this temporary journey on earth. The Designer knew when we left the factory that worry is destructive. The study above merely confirms what Jesus said a couple of millennia ago:

> That is why I tell you not to worry about everyday life—whether you have enough food and drink, or enough clothes to wear. Isn't life more than food, and your body more than clothing? Look at the birds. They don't plant or harvest or store food in barns, for your heavenly Father feeds them. And aren't you far more valuable to him than they are? Can all your worries add a single moment to your life?
>
> MATTHEW 6:25-27

Worries certainly cannot add a moment, though it appears they can subtract. Jesus continues in the same message:

> So don't worry about these things, saying, "What will we eat? What will we drink? What will we wear?" These

things dominate the thoughts of unbelievers, but your heavenly Father already knows all your needs. Seek the Kingdom of God above all else, and live righteously, and he will give you everything you need. So don't worry about tomorrow, for tomorrow will bring its own worries. Today's trouble is enough for today.

MATTHEW 6:31-34

Our Designer knew something else. Most of what we consume ourselves with never happens or is not worth getting agitated about. Again, modern research comes along to verify ancient wisdom.

A Cornell University research study examined how many times an imagined calamity actually came to pass. In this study, subjects were asked to write down their worries over an extended period of time, and then identify which of their imagined misfortunes did not actually happen.

The results were remarkable—85 percent of what subjects worried about never happened! Slow down and digest that. Eighty-five percent of what we work ourselves into varied states of frenzy about *never even happens*. And here is what is more remarkable. For the 15 percent of the worry agenda that did happen, nearly 80 percent of the respondents reported they were able to deal with the concern better than expected or they learned a valuable lesson from the event. So 97 percent of what the majority of this study group worried about was not worth wasting the energy, faith, and time on.[1]

Today's grace suggestion is not easy, but it could be an important step forward.

Living in fear of the future cheats you out of today. A precious moment tugs on your heart like a child at your sleeve. Too often you stub your toe on that sacred moment while concerning yourself with something that won't happen or will happen in a way that your worry cannot change. That is exactly where the enemy wants to keep you and me as children of God, with our eyes on worry and not on God.

Trusting Jesus for tomorrow, next week, next year, and forever frees us to see what this moment holds. Poet Maya Angelou said, "We spend precious hours fearing the inevitable. It would be wise to use that time adoring our families, cherishing our friends and living our lives."

Indeed. The inevitable is, well, inevitable. No amount of worry will change the fact that we will face sadness, adversity, and death, a huge challenge for most of us. I have seen how worry consumes those I love. My ever-worrying dad used to remark that I was not a worrier. I would respond with a smile on my face. "I know you're on that job, Dad, so I don't need to duplicate your efforts."

If I do struggle with worry, I remember that my heavenly Father is on the job, not as a worrier, but calling me to know Him, trust Him, and rest in Him. I can safely give my worries to God. If I can remind myself when worry prevails *that God is for me and that He loves me*, then I can trust Him with tomorrow and beyond.

> Jesus said, "Come to me, all of you who are weary and carry heavy burdens, and I will give you rest. Take my yoke upon you. Let me teach you, because I am humble and gentle at heart, and you will find rest for your souls. For my yoke is easy to bear, and the burden I give you is light."
>
> MATTHEW 11:28-30

A story about an English movie executive might offer some practical application for us. J. Arthur Rank was worrying himself into ulcers, so he decided to pick Wednesday as the day he would worry. On the other days of the week, whatever came up that was worrisome was written down and placed in his worry box. On each Wednesday he would open the box to read the slips of paper. A most interesting thing happened. Rank found that most of the things that had triggered potential worries had been resolved within the week and it would have been pointless to have worried about them.[2]

Worry robs us of the strength to address daily problems. Worry causes me to take my eyes off the source of my strength—Jesus. *He is my strength and my hope.* If I keep my eyes on Jesus, the words of a classic hymn will begin to ring true in my heart:

> *Turn your eyes upon Jesus,*
> *Look full in His wonderful face,*
> *And the things of earth will grow strangely dim,*
> *In the light of His glory and grace.*[3]

All of us deal with worry. There is no sin in that. But we have a Friend who never deserts us and never grows weary of our needs. Remember who walks beside you and share— actually, *give* those worries to Him. Your life is a tapestry of moments woven in the now. Don't miss a special moment worrying about something that may not happen and will not happen without the knowledge of your heavenly Father.

Application postscript: God has interesting timing. I had just hit "save" and "print" to review this chapter about worrying when the phone rang. My dermatologist was calling with the results of a biopsy taken on my face. Here is the transcript as my brain heard it:

Your biopsy on your temple was squamous cell **CANCER**. The good news is that this type of **CANCER** is very slow growing. But you will need Mohs **SURGERY** to remove it.

I know this is the result of many summers of sun exposure. I know the procedure is routine. Of course, it is always routine until it is your face getting cut! This is one more reminder of how things can change in a heartbeat. This call was pretty minor. The next one may not be. But my conviction is that I can handle whatever comes my way, if I keep focused on my Source of strength. No use to worry with Jesus at my side. We've got this. The two of you can handle life's challenges as well! No worries.

Postscript to the postscript: Everything went just fine with the surgery. In keeping with our hope to find blessings in weird places, I offer this: the doctor was able to make the incision to remove the skin cancer along one of my laugh/wrinkle lines, so the scar doesn't show at all! Those well-earned wrinkles are finally paying off!

GOD'S TAKE

[Jesus promised,] "I am leaving you with
a gift—peace of mind and heart. And
the peace I give is a gift the world cannot
give. So don't be troubled or afraid."

JOHN 14:27

A DOSE OF GRACE

Recognize your worries without shame and without feeling that you are spiritually weak. Worry and fear are tools of the enemy to keep us from focusing on Jesus and His gift of peace of mind and heart. Maybe try the "worry box" for a few weeks. God has this! Leave your worries with God, and enjoy the blessings of today.

CHAPTER 12

KINDNESS REALLY IS CONTAGIOUS

The greatest thing a man can do for his Heavenly Father
is to be kind to some of His other children.

HENRY DRUMMOND

Recently, Joni and I took a field trip with our grandkiddos to the Gentle Zoo in Forney, Texas. It is a fun and kid-friendly place that is home to a menagerie of critters including pigs, ducks, cows, goats, peacocks, chickens, and horses.

It was a nice respite from city sounds to hear the chorus of bleating, whinnying, oinking, and clucking. We bought a container of food for the animals, and as soon as we approached, hopeful animals headed in our direction. The residents clearly knew the drill.

Clara's favorite animals were the goats. They pushed their noses through the fence of their outdoor home. Clara was fearless as she petted and fed the sweet goats that gently took the food out of her hand. Not so sweet was a slightly overbearing llama that forced its way into almost every feeding opportunity.

We had been warned that this critter was harmless but occasionally could get a little grumpy. I understand that completely. The employee said llamas rarely spit at people, but if you see their ears pinned back, and they're staring at you, avoid eye contact and act nonthreatening. That has always been my strategy on the subway in New York, so this was an easy plan to implement. Since llamas can spit as far as ten feet away, I was quite mindful of the no-eye-contact rule.

As we wandered among the various animal enclosures, a sign posted on the grounds caught my eye:

> We believe everyone deserves a second chance. In fact, many of our animal ambassadors have been rescued and adopted from shelters, private homes and sanctuaries in Texas. Though they come to us with a sad story, they are now loving and caring examples of what compassion and confidence can do.

It made the trip more special to know that many of the animals had been rescued from abusive or neglectful situations. Kindness had rescued them. Knowing that, I even had to give the llama a bit of grace, while still keeping a respectful distance. Isn't that a pretty good picture of the gospel of grace? Most of us have some sad stories that we would love to have redeemed in a compassionate second chance. We get that second chance through Christ, and when that happens, we also become ambassadors of compassion.

We are Christ's ambassadors; God is making his appeal through us. We speak for Christ when we plead, "Come back to God!"

2 CORINTHIANS 5:20

I especially related to this additional information on the zoo sign:

Many of our critters have been disabled or injured prior to arriving at the Gentle Zoo. With a little love and care they can thrive despite their disabilities.

That pretty much describes the résumé I brought to Jesus when I recognized my need for something or someone bigger than myself. I was a hurtin' critter disabled by sin and injured by life. Jesus gave me not a little but a *lot* of love and kindness, along with a bonus helping of forgiveness and grace.

The amazing thing about God's grace is that He is not a God of a second chance. He is a God of chance after chance after chance ad infinitum. We are never outside God's redeeming grace, no matter how much or how often we blow it.

How is that even possible? We write off people after one or two offenses. How can God keep forgiving us after countless offenses? It doesn't make sense. That is because grace does not make sense in our accounting system. So how does that work in our relationships with our community? The apostle Paul pulls it all together perfectly in his letter to the church in Ephesus:

Instead, be kind to each other, tenderhearted, forgiving one another, just as God through Christ has forgiven you.

EPHESIANS 4:32

Kindness should be contagious because the God of the universe has been kind to us. That is part and parcel of the love story of the gospel.

> Don't you see how wonderfully kind, tolerant, and patient God is with you? Does this mean nothing to you? Can't you see that his kindness is intended to turn you from your sin?
>
> ROMANS 2:4

I used to be impressed by talent and prestige. Now I find that I am more impressed by kindness. Billy Graham observed how we all—especially children—benefit from a little kindness: "Often the only thing a child can remember about an adult in later years, when he or she is grown, is whether or not that person was kind."[1] I find that to be so true when I run down the list of adults from my childhood. I filter them by that very trait. They were either kind or unkind.

My memories from high school have changed too. I once sorted classmates by prettiness and athletic ability. Now I sort my high school acquaintances by kindness. All the things that identified us in high school are meaningless now. Who cares if you were a cheerleader, quarterback, National Merit scholar, or the kid trying to find someone to sit with at lunch? What matters is whether you were kind and considerate of others. I spent my high school years walking a tightrope, trying to be part of the "in" group, while trying to live out my newfound faith in Jesus. If I failed to be kind in that awkward dance, I am truly sorry.

Paul recognized the importance of this contagious gift in his instructions to the church at Colossae:

Since God chose you to be the holy people he loves, you must clothe yourselves with tenderhearted mercy, kindness, humility, gentleness, and patience. Make allowance for each other's faults, and forgive anyone who offends you. Remember, the Lord forgave you, so you must forgive others. Above all, clothe yourselves with love, which binds us all together in perfect harmony. And let the peace that comes from Christ rule in your hearts. For as members of one body you are called to live in peace. And always be thankful.

COLOSSIANS 3:12-15

I have often said that if the church lived according to those four verses alone, there would be a spiritual awakening in the land. If we simply loved one another in the body of Christ, we could spark a revival. That is my job as a follower of Christ.

We are the hands, feet, and arms of God on this planet. Christian group Casting Crowns asked lyrically, "If we are the body, why aren't His arms reaching? Why aren't His hands healing?"[2] I am afraid the answer is a hard truth.

Recently, as I walked down the streets of a major city and saw dozens of homeless people, I realized I care far more about my comfort and safety than I do about lonely people's needs. Yes, I know it sometimes feels overwhelming when I see such vast needs and incredible suffering. But I can do something. I can climb out of my cozy Christian bubble and get a little dirty right where I am.

For me, this means being available when my coworkers and friends are going through a valley. It is a hard thing to speak regularly with someone who has been disappointed by

God, life, and others. Perhaps I am not having a mountain-top experience myself, and it can be a challenge to hear the hurt and anger in their voices. They pour out their pain, and I often have nothing to offer other than a listening ear, a caring heart, prayer, and presence. Remarkably, God seems to use those simple acts of kindness.

Sometimes I feel overwhelmed. Sometimes I think it is a hopeless world we live in. But I can do something. I can be kind. Edward Everett Hale once said, "I am only one; but still I am one. I cannot do everything, but still I can do something; I will not refuse to do something I can do."

I am not trying to shovel guilt on you or myself. Maybe we should be more intentional about *being* the body of Christ, rather than relying on government programs to do our job for us. I want the grace that God has given me to make my heart sensitive toward the poor as well as toward hurting and spiritually seeking people. It is hard to spend much time in the New Testament and not realize our challenge to be the body of Christ. Here is a *very small* sample:

> If anyone has the world's goods and sees his brother in need, yet closes his heart against him, how does God's love abide in him?
>
> I JOHN 3:17, ESV

> What good is it, my brothers, if someone says he has faith but does not have works? Can that faith save him? If a brother or sister is poorly clothed and lacking in daily food, and one of you says to them, "Go in peace, be warmed and filled," without giving them the things needed for the body, what good is that? So also faith by itself, if it does not have works, is dead.
>
> JAMES 2:14-17, ESV

[Jesus] answered, "You shall love the Lord your God with all your heart and with all your soul and with all your strength and with all your mind, and your neighbor as yourself."

LUKE 10:27, ESV

There was not a needy person among them, for as many as were owners of lands or houses sold them and brought the proceeds of what was sold and laid it at the apostles' feet, and it was distributed to each as any had need. Thus Joseph, who was also called by the apostles Barnabas (which means son of encouragement), a Levite, a native of Cyprus, sold a field that belonged to him and brought the money and laid it at the apostles' feet.

ACTS 4:34-37, ESV

Let each of you look not only to his own interests, but also to the interests of others.

PHILIPPIANS 2:4, ESV

The charge of hypocrisy leveled at the church has a lot to do with our obsession with sin management over living a life of kindness, grace, and service. If I am not living out of grace, then Jesus' arms aren't reaching as far as they could through me. Kindness is clearly step one.

What if God's people really cared? What if I really cared? Wouldn't it make a difference? I remember how much Joni and I were impacted by acts of kindness during her cancer battle. Friends Bob and Mary Word found out that one of the few things that tasted good to Joni after chemotherapy was tomato basil soup and saltines. So every week we would find a care package of soup and saltines on our porch. Ronnie and Carol Goldman drove the one-and-a-half-hour jaunt from their Fort Worth home to our house, pulled up, handed us a delicious dinner, and drove home. They knew we had little energy for social interaction, but they wanted to show their love.

I remember one night well into the cancer-treatment journey. Joni was feeling particularly down. If anyone had called wanting to visit, she would have said no, not tonight. Then, without notice, the Keener kids—Hannah, Rebecca, Noah, and Jonah—surprised us with hugs and gifts, infusing a sad atmosphere with kindness and love. God knew that's what Joni needed. She calls that moment and so many others postcards from God, and they seemed to be delivered at the most appropriate times.

Straight-talking James writes that "to one who knows the right thing to do and does not do it, to him it is sin" (James 4:17, NASB).

I cannot argue that I do not know the right thing to do. My response will reveal my heart.

In research done by Darley and Batson at Princeton in 1973, a group of theology students received the assignment to walk across campus and present a sermon about the Good Samaritan.

> As part of the research, some of these students were told that they were late and needed to hurry up. Along their route across campus, Darley and Baston had hired an actor to play the role of a victim who was coughing and suffering.
>
> Ninety percent of the "late" students in Princeton Theology Seminary ignored the needs of the suffering person in their haste to get across campus. As the study reports, "Indeed, on several occasions,

a seminary student going to give his talk on the
parable of the Good Samaritan literally stepped over
the victim as he hurried on his way!"[3]

How many times have I stepped over a person in need, as
I rushed to do "ministry"? My default thinking needs to pose
this question: What will happen to a needy soul if, at the very
least, I can't offer that person kindness?

Ready for a little more conviction from marriage expert
John Gottman? (To be honest, I didn't know there was such
a profession.) He looked for the presence of kindness or
contempt in marriage relationships. Here's what the research
uncovered in an article published in the *Atlantic*:

> *Contempt . . . is the number one factor that tears
> couples apart.* People who are focused on criticizing
> their partners miss a whopping 50 percent of
> positive things their partners are doing and they
> see negativity when it's not there. People who
> give their partner the cold shoulder—deliberately
> ignoring the partner or responding minimally—
> damage the relationship by making their partner feel
> worthless and invisible, as if they're not there, not
> valued. And people who treat their partners with
> contempt and criticize them not only kill the love
> in the relationship, but they also kill their partner's
> ability to fight off viruses and cancers. Being mean
> is the death knell of relationships.
> *Kindness, on the other hand, glues couples together.*
> Research independent from theirs has shown that
> kindness is [one of] the most important predictors
> of satisfaction and stability in a marriage. Kindness

makes each partner feel cared for, understood, and validated—feel loved. . . . There's a great deal of evidence showing the more someone receives or witnesses kindness, the more they will be kind themselves, which leads to upward spirals of love and generosity in a relationship.[4]

The same principles apply to parenting, the workplace, the church, and the community. Contempt tears us apart, but kindness glues us together. And kindness is contagious. Joni and I are very different, and we often joke that the matchmaking services would never have put us together. But we have made it work, and understanding and accepting each other's differences has been key. When we accept those differences, we also begin to see how God uses our unique giftedness to balance out each other.

Kindness doesn't require great skill or advanced degrees. I can be kind with a PhD or a GED. I do not have to like someone to be kind. I have to remember that kindness means disconnecting from devices, so I can actually see and react to those around me. Kindness is powerful. Kindness tears down walls. Kindness builds trust.

Kindness shows the love of Christ through my imperfect efforts. As a Christian, kindness gives those I encounter a reason to listen to my message of redemption and grace. In return, I will be changed, receiving the greater gift.

I think writer Alexander MacLaren summarized it beautifully: "Kindness makes a person attractive. If you would win the world, melt it, do not hammer it."

GOD'S TAKE

Give thanks to the LORD, for he is good!
His faithful love endures forever.

PSALM 107:1

A DOSE OF GRACE

Be contagious with kindness. Infect your world, and practice kindness every chance that you get. Note the response of those you extend it to. Theologian Frederick Buechner captured the idea brilliantly: "If you want to be holy, be kind." Anyone can do it. Intentional acts of kindness will return more than you can imagine. Give it a try.

CHAPTER 13

DARE *NOT* TO COMPARE

Comparison is the thief of joy.

THEODORE ROOSEVELT

I WAS BLESSED TO WORK WITH two Christian leaders with the Dallas Mavericks when I moved to the area in 1980. General manager Norm Sonju taught me to be thorough, prepared, and never satisfied with the status quo. His drive for excellence made me much better at my job. Business manager Paul Phipps was my immediate boss. Paul always had our backs as a part of his team, so it surprised me when he said to our staff, "There is one thing that will get you fired right away."

My mind raced as he paused for effect. Laziness? Insubordination? Lying?

"If I hear that you are comparing your salaries, you will be fired."

I am not sure if that was a real threat or a ploy to get our attention, but with Paul you didn't test the waters. His point was that comparing only leads to envy, dissension, and disunity. Later I asked him for more clarity about this somewhat surprising ultimatum.

"It is entirely up to the organization to determine the value and resulting compensation you bring," he said. "If you feel you are being underpaid, the conversation should be with management and not with your fellow employees."

I have never forgotten that lesson about the power of comparison to disrupt a group of men and women working together. I just wish I would have transferred that lesson more effectively to my personal life when it comes to comparing my skills to the skill sets of others.

When a group of men get together and start sharing stories, I get nervous. If the topic is sports, I'm good. If the conversation drifts toward hunting or fishing, I can bluff my way through it. A turn to current events is good for me too. But if the conversation turns to home-repair projects, I get an immediate case of low T. Just this past week a friend was talking about fixing the heating element in the dryer and replacing some apparently vital part on his home air conditioner. I could not have been more out of my comfort zone.

One of my favorite comedians, Mike Birbiglia, has a very funny line about what happens to him when asked to dance. "I went to a dance club the other day, which was timely because my self-esteem had been hovering around normal, and I'd been meaning to knock it down to negative one thousand."[1]

As I've confessed, I personally relate to that feeling when something quits working at my home. I was not blessed with the handyman gene, and those who have it seem remarkably condescending to those who don't. They proclaim how easy every project is.

No, it's not!

Women brag about how handy and helpful their husbands are around the house. "Jim just repaired a slab leak by drilling through the bathroom floor, repairing the plumbing, and retiling the floor." My biggest home repair in recent memory was replacing a flapper on the toilet, and that took two attempts.

I get absolutely green with envy when I watch men and women effortlessly tear apart and repair things. I can execute only the tearing-apart step. I have learned to save time by just calling the plumber, carpenter, or mechanic first. I feel the superior smirks of these folks performing, in their world, the simplest of tasks as I watch miserably. I want to drag them to my workplace and show them I am competent at something, but instead I write a check and mumble an embarrassed thank-you. Sometimes I talk about football to show them I like masculine things. How sad is that?

But that is what happens when you play the no-win game of comparison. We all do it. Comparison is poison to the soul. I either contrast myself to someone doing something better than me and feel downcast, or I measure myself to someone failing and feel better. Sometimes I even secretly wish that person would fail so I can feel better about my efforts.

Perhaps that is my cue to refer to the Instruction Manual again. Paul writes about this very problem that was happening in the church at Corinth:

> Oh, don't worry; we wouldn't dare say that we are as wonderful as these other men who tell you how important they are! But they are only comparing themselves with each other, using themselves as the standard of measurement. How ignorant!

2 CORINTHIANS 10:12

Writer Ann Voskamp notes that we try to measure how we are doing with imperfect—and even dangerous—measuring sticks:

> Measuring sticks try to rank some people as big and some people as small—but we aren't sizes. We are souls. *There are no better people or worse people—there are only God-made souls.* There is no point trying to size people up, no point trying to compare—because *souls defy measuring.*[2]

At the beginning of this book I quoted Psalm 139, detailing how God uniquely wove together each of our individual DNA to create the one and only me and the one and only you.

He knew us before we were formed, and He has ordained our days. Paul unpacks that even more in Ephesians:

> It's in Christ that we find out who we are and what we are living for. Long before we first heard of Christ and got our hopes up, he had his eye on us, had designs on us for glorious living, part of the overall purpose he is working out in everything and everyone.
>
> EPHESIANS 1:11-12, MSG

I am not an accident. I have a purpose in God's plan. I have a role in God's overall purpose. And I have a specific calling as a gift of grace.

> God saved us and called us to live a holy life. He did this, not because we deserved it, but because that was

his plan from before the beginning of time—to show us his grace through Christ Jesus.

2 TIMOTHY 1:9

Each one of us is distinctive and needed in God's community. But I often don't feel that way and generally don't live that way. Part of the problem is that I compare my talents and gifts to others'. There is a long list of gifts I wish I had. Musical talent. Athletic ability. Handyman skills. But I am uniquely me, and I am needed in the body of Christ for it to be complete. And so are you.

Paul compares our various gifts to the human body. We are not whole without eyes, ears, feet, or hands. Other hidden parts of the body have vital functions that go unnoticed. Yet every part of the body has a role, and Paul is simply saying that we often value the parts of the body without perspective.

Our bodies have many parts, and God has put each part just where he wants it. How strange a body would be if it had only one part! Yes, there are many parts, but only one body. The eye can never say to the hand, "I don't need you." The head can't say to the feet, "I don't need you."

In fact, some parts of the body that seem weakest and least important are actually the most necessary.

1 CORINTHIANS 12:18-22

We don't think much about the thyroid. Most of us have no idea how vital that little gland is to normal living until something goes awry. That is Paul's point. Every part of the body, glamorous and unglamorous, is vital to the health of the human body.

If one part suffers, all the parts suffer with it, and if one part is honored, all the parts are glad.

I CORINTHIANS 12:26

At least that's how it's supposed to work. The body takes a lot of parts to be whole, and some get more attention than others. I am not particularly interested in being the lower digestive tract of the body. I want to be the brain or the lightning-fast legs. But the truth is that when the lower digestive tract is in distress, the brain can think of nothing else and immediately marshals all resources to provide possible relief. The lightning-fast legs are interested only in racing to one location. When a part of the physical anatomy suffers, the entire body suffers as well. That is what Paul is communicating. We all have a role, and comparison calls into question the wisdom of the Creator who designed us with deliberate intention and for specific roles in His plan. When I compare and find myself lacking, I am questioning my Creator and His unique design for me.

Being content with who you are really is a heart issue grounded in the truth of who you are according to Scripture. How I wish that I could see myself as God sees me. Because of what Christ did on my behalf, God sees me as a saint. Forgiven. Valuable. Needed. What I often see is the same old failure who can't dance, fix anything, or live consistently for God.

My fears about my shortcomings are confirmed when I log in to Facebook and Instagram and see the smiling perfection of many of my friends. I am psychologically wired toward social comparisons, and social media is exactly the wrong medicine for that predisposition. Facebook is not a real representation of life. It is a carefully controlled résumé of often-phony "moments."

We see those smiling families and couples and think they are experiencing some alternate life that has eluded us. I'm sorry to break the news, but there are no perfect people or perfect families.

Someone recently told me that a hurting friend was not comfortable sharing his trials with me because I had, in his mind, a perfect marriage and family. You would have much better odds finding Sasquatch than a truly perfect marriage and family—including mine. It does not exist. But the enemy loves to point out that your marriage or job or house doesn't match your hopes or expectations, especially when set side by side with others. That is why honest communication in community is so vital to being a healthy follower of Jesus.

Recently Joni and I met with a young couple who are going through the normal stuff that couples go through. We shared with them about the difficult seasons we went through. Joni honestly shared how hard it was to have a husband too absorbed in work to be present for her. We talked about the tipping point where we (mainly me) had to decide to change or give up. We committed to each other, and God has redeemed that decision over and over. Invariably this honest conversation will garner this response:

"Really? We thought you guys had a perfect marriage."

What we have is a perfect Savior who longs for us to trust Him and commit to one another for better or for worse. I am pretty sure I said those very words forty-something years ago, but much of that day is a blur. This is what Joni and I can say without hesitation after decades together: "Persevere, because it is so worth it. It won't be easy, to be sure. But something of such great value is rarely easy."

Trying to be the "perfect" and "together" Christian is really pervasive in the church. Have you ever done this? You are angry, petty, and bitter during the week, or even on the way to church. As soon as you walk through the church door, you are beaming and waving like a homecoming queen. We can fool the congregation, but we cannot fool the Creator.

The fellowship of believers should be a place where honesty is encouraged, where shortcomings are accepted. Where the part of the body that is hurting can tell the rest of the body that they need help. Church should be the place where you can say without fear, "I am struggling; I hurt; I need you." But for some reason the opposite happens far too often. People who are really in pain have this conversation every week in churches across this land:

"How are you doing?" (insincere query, because they are too wounded to really care)

"Great, how are you?" (dishonest reply, followed by perfunctory courtesy question)

"Fantastic, great to see you." (really dishonest reply, with a safe dismissal salutation)

Am I advocating dumping our hurts on everyone we meet? Of course not. I know that too many have been wounded by unsafe places. That breaks my heart. But there are rooms of grace that exist. Don't give up. Please.

My fear is that we have created a culture where we feel there is something wrong with us if we are hurting. If I am struggling, I must be doing something wrong spiritually. Shouldn't God meet this need? What is wrong with me? The fact that God created me with a desire to be in community tells me that part of His plan is for me to be helped by other members of the body of Christ. But I think I am falling short by comparing myself to false images of people who are not being real.

Anne Lamott weighs in with her typical, unvarnished honesty: "Everyone is screwed up, broken, clingy, and scared, even the people who seem to have it more or less together. They are much more like you than you would believe. So try not to compare your insides to their outsides."[3]

Being broken, clingy, scared, and screwed up is spiritual soil prep for the seed of grace to grow.

Yet for years I chose to stay hidden. Satan convinced me that I would be rejected if I dared to let others see the truth behind the person. To be honest, I have been wounded at times by unkind folks. But I want to be willing to take a chance to be real. I want to be authentic and see where that takes me, no matter the risk.

What does honest and real community look like? Here is one example:

> Let us consider how we may spur one another on
> toward love and good deeds, not giving up meeting
> together, as some are in the habit of doing, but
> encouraging one another—and all the more as you
> see the Day approaching.
>
> HEBREWS 10:24-25, NIV

When someone in the body achieves or creates something that I wish I had accomplished, I must not shrink in comparison. I should celebrate that person, thank God for the contribution to the body, and remember that I also have a vital part in this plan.

I am not sure if writer John Mason had a biblical worldview

in mind when he came up with the title for his book *You're Born an Original, Don't Die a Copy*, but he is theologically spot on. We are uniquely and completely designed for our roles in the body of Christ. Don't try to imitate another part.

The biggest danger to missing our lines in the production called life is comparison. Relax and be you. No one compares to you!

GOD'S TAKE

Don't be selfish; don't try to impress others. Be humble, thinking of others as better than yourselves. Don't look out only for your own interests, but take an interest in others, too.

PHILIPPIANS 2:3-4

A DOSE OF GRACE

Accept who you are and your role in the body of Christ. Don't try to be something you are not. And if you are not sure that you are important in God's plan, then you are not hearing His voice on the matter. Meditate on how you contribute to the body of believers and your community. Tell God that you are content with your role and that you are grateful for the gifts you have been given. Ask Him to make you aware of how to distribute them generously.

CHAPTER 14

IF YOU'RE HAPPY
AND YOU KNOW IT . . .

Happiness is like a butterfly which, when pursued, is always beyond
our grasp, but, if you will sit down quietly, may alight upon you.

NATHANIEL HAWTHORNE

I WAS FEELING A LITTLE MELANCHOLY in the middle of a long baseball road trip. Suddenly, my phone lit up with a FaceTime request. The Waco number made me smile in anticipation because one of my grandchildren would soon be on the line. Usually it is an exuberant report from grandson Ethan about some event he attended.

This time when the video call connected, there was a beautiful little one-year-old girl standing proudly with a beatific smile. Madeline. She was cute as could be in her plaid dress. Her dad, Matt, reported that Madeline was standing all on her own and was taking some tentative steps. She was obviously proud of herself and loving her new skill.

Then she saw my face and heard my voice. She started to

giggle. I laughed and did my Papa thing, making all kinds of faces and silly noises. She giggled some more. I laughed some more. Whatever negative things may have transpired up to that call were swept away in that moment of precious interaction. I can still picture the delight on her face as I write these words.

Wait, you say. You're using your phone?

Yes, this sacred moment was made possible by technology, which I'm extremely grateful for, since my grandchildren are growing up way too fast. Just to clarify, these devices are not inherently bad. They are just one more thing we must prioritize. Devices are a good thing that we must zealously guard from becoming an ultimate thing.

Sometimes it takes a toddler to teach you the importance of laughter. After all, it is such an important tool in this journey to live more fully in each day we are given. Life is hard. That very information is found in the Owner's Manual. The Bible is very clear that life will be a journey of highs and lows. Solomon described these as seasons of our lives:

> A time to cry and a time to laugh.
> A time to grieve and a time to dance.
> ECCLESIASTES 3:4

God has given us a wonderful asset for such times that we too often leave unopened: the gift of laughter. I believe a sense of humor is one of God's most precious provisions to help us make it through this life. Does God laugh? I believe He does. We are created in the very image of God, and laughter is a big part of who we are. There is an old saying that says if you want to make God laugh, just tell Him your plans. The Bible does not say that God reacts by writing "LOL" in the clouds, but it does paint a picture of a God who exults in His children with phrases like this:

> Then God will rejoice over you
>   as a bridegroom rejoices over his bride.
> ISAIAH 62:5

When a bridegroom rejoices over his bride, there is laughter and fun. When God delights in us, I picture Him expressing that kind of joy.

One of the really sad cultural messages that the church has communicated is that Jesus was a humorless prophet preaching repentance to a world of shamed and wretched sinners. I believe that Jesus was a warm, vibrant messenger of God's redemptive plan to people who needed a Savior. I think Jesus had to have been engaging, dynamic, and funny. How else could you explain the massive crowds, devoted followers, and lasting impact He had in three short years?

When I consulted the World Catalog of Books last November, I found that 466,236 books (give or take a couple) had been written about Jesus. When I narrowed that search to "Jesus' sense of humor," the number went down to 98.[1] And when I started wading through those book titles, I saw only a handful of them were written solely about Jesus and His humor. One unlikely writer reflecting on Jesus' humor was noted Quaker preacher Elton Trueblood, who said, "We should never trust a theologian who doesn't have a sense of humor." I would have to agree.

Miserable Christians are a poor selling point for the joyous truths of grace. We proclaim that we are offering Good News with a face that looks like the dog just ran away. Where did we get this idea that following Jesus means the end of fun? Puritan (yes, Puritan) John Calvin writes, "We are nowhere forbidden to laugh, or to be full, or to add new to old or hereditary possessions, or to be satisfied with food, or delighted by music, or to drink wine."[2]

Actually, in my early church experience, I was forbidden from pretty much that whole list. No wonder those outside of faith look at Christianity like submitting to a good-times lobotomy. But that is just one more lie about real faith.

Recently I was with Ethan, who was sad about something that had not gone according to his plan. I went all in to make him smile. He temporarily broke his mood with a smile and then caught himself.

"Papa! Quit trying to make me laugh."

That was like waving a red cape in front of a bull. I tripled down on silly Papa antics. Ethan knew he could not hold out, so he threw this out: "Papa! Just act like a normal human."

Ethan apparently believes in miracles. But I was unrelenting, and he soon cheered up to his normal, happy self.

The authors of the Gospels were not inspired to write a humor volume, so you won't find snappy one-liners from Jesus. But you will find examples of humor and sarcasm in His words. Yes, He was completely divine, but He also was a normal human being and acted so. Imagine the looks on the faces of the disciples when they breathlessly informed Jesus that He had stirred up trouble.

> "Did you know how upset the Pharisees were when they heard what you said?"
> MATTHEW 15:12, MSG

I am sure they expected Him to show concern and wonder how He could repair the damage with these important leaders.

"Forget them. They are blind men leading blind men.
When a blind man leads a blind man, they both end up
in the ditch."

MATTHEW 15:14, MSG

Can't you imagine Jesus' answer catching the disciples
unawares, first surprising and then cracking them up? I
would have been grinning if I had been there.

Jesus received invitations to weddings and banquets and
private dinners, all of which riled up the Pharisees' jealousy
and drew their judgment. Would Jesus be invited to multiple
wedding feasts if he were a self-righteous and dour stick in
the mud? It is clear that He was a welcome guest. Luke tells
us about one such gathering:

> Levi gave a large dinner at his home for Jesus.
> Everybody was there, tax men and other disreputable
> characters as guests at the dinner. The Pharisees and
> their religion scholars came to his disciples greatly
> offended. "What is he doing eating and drinking with
> crooks and 'sinners'?"
>
> Jesus heard about it and spoke up, "Who needs
> a doctor: the healthy or the sick? I'm here inviting
> outsiders, not insiders—an invitation to a changed life,
> changed inside and out."
>
> They asked him, "John's disciples are well-known
> for keeping fasts and saying prayers. Also the Pharisees.
> But you seem to spend most of your time at parties.
> Why?"
>
> Jesus said, "When you're celebrating a wedding, you
> don't skimp on the cake and wine. You feast. Later you
> may need to pull in your belt, but this isn't the time. As

long as the bride and groom are with you, you have a good time."

LUKE 5:29-34, MSG

Our portrayals of Jesus with a sad or angry countenance are completely blown away by these passages. Jesus delighted in celebrating, and those around Him obviously enjoyed His company. Jesus knew that those who most needed the touch of forgiveness might not be hanging around the religious types.

Now consider the men that Jesus chose to live His life with for three years. It is probable that six or seven of the apostles were fishermen. Throw in a hated tax collector. The professions of the other four are not known. If you have been part of a group of working men, you would suspect this might be an occasionally crass group. I would doubt that the ribald sense of humor possessed by these common men suddenly became sanctimonious introspection when they decided to follow Jesus. In fact, I would venture a guess that Jesus would not have wanted that to happen. One of the most important elements of bonding together is laughing and sharing fun experiences as a group. I believe that Jesus and the twelve sat around the fire at night laughing and telling stories on one another.

I work in television. The language that surrounds me is not always edifying, but I don't suck the air out of the TV truck with self-righteous indignation. Sometimes my workmate Carla will kiddingly say, "Welcome to your nurturing, spiritual environment, Dave." I just smile. I love my TV family.

Laughter is a surprisingly complex commodity. I have to pursue it. I have to invite it. I have to allow it a place at the table. This quote attributed to Benjamin Franklin sums it up: "The Constitution only guarantees the American people the right to pursue happiness. You have to catch it yourself."

Jesus recognized that there would be times of sorrow but that God would also bless us with laughter.

God blesses you who weep now,
    for in due time you will laugh.
LUKE 6:21

The wisdom of Proverbs clearly touts the benefits of laughter and happiness.

A glad heart makes a happy face;
    a broken heart crushes the spirit.
PROVERBS 15:13

For the despondent, every day brings trouble;
    for the happy heart, life is a continual feast.
PROVERBS 15:15

Need some convincing data of the Bible's insight into our souls? Here are some highlights of two studies on the positive effects of laughter.

Loma Linda University studied healthy people in their sixties and seventies to gauge the impact of humor on memory recall. One group remained silent, while the other group watched funny videos. Afterward, the humor group not only did significantly better on memory recall but the stress hormone cortisol was considerably lowered.[3]

The Mayo Clinic found that laughter boosts the immune system by releasing neuropeptides that help fight stress and aid in preventing potentially more serious illnesses.[4]

Recently we traveled to share a special event with our dear friends Ed and Judy Underwood, who live in California. It was a bit of a last-minute decision, and we were so excited to join them. They eagerly volunteered to pick us up at Ontario International Airport. Our flight was delayed a bit, so I sent a few status updates. After a couple of those notifications, Judy replied, "Ed is tracking your flight."

I took that to mean I could cease and desist from the estimated flight-arrival reports. Our plane landed a few minutes earlier than expected, and we shot a quick text that our flight had landed. We deplaned and looked around for our friends. When we didn't see them, we figured they were probably parked in the cell phone waiting lot or circling the airport waiting for our text. We went outside to look. No sign of them.

I sent another text asking if they were nearby, and I received this response: "Be there soon. We are caught in traffic."

Ontario International Airport has very unique benches with rounded backs in the baggage claim area, making them uncomfortable to sit on. The airport personnel clearly do not want stragglers hanging out on benches. Joni and I sat down on the humpbacked bench with our luggage next to us.

"This is not exactly the way I pictured this," I said.

Joni responded with a laugh. "I feel valued."

"I'm glad Ed was tracking the flight."

We started laughing more, and then Joni offered this gem: "I would lay down, but I would just roll off of this bench."

When we finally rendezvoused with Ed and Judy, they found us laughing. Soon we were all laughing. That is what friends do. You laugh together.

Laughter makes you feel better—it's a medical fact.

In an article for *National Geographic*, Michael Miller, director of the Center for Preventive Cardiology at the University of Maryland Medical Center in Baltimore, explains, "A good belly laugh leads to the release of endorphins from the brain." This causes nitric oxide to widen blood vessels, which increases blood flow and reduces inflammation and cholesterol plaque formation.

The articles continues, "A 2005 study by Miller measured the blood flow of 20 volunteers before and after watching a funny movie and a sad movie. After the sad movie, blood flow was more restricted in 14 of the 20 viewers. But after seeing the movie that made them laugh, average blood flow increased by 22 percent." Miller goes so far as to prescribe fifteen minutes of daily laughter for heart health. That is my kind of doctor![5]

Even if your results vary, there can be no real downside to laughing daily.

So once again the Instruction Manual is spot on.

A cheerful disposition is good for your health;
gloom and doom leave you bone-tired.
PROVERBS 17:22, MSG

An intriguing UC–Berkeley thirty-year longitudinal study examined the smiles of students pictured in an old yearbook and measured their well-being and success throughout their lives. By measuring the smiles in the photographs, the researchers were able to predict a number of things: how fulfilling and long lasting their marriages would be, how highly they would score on standardized tests of well-being and general happiness, and how inspiring they would be to others. The widest smilers consistently ranked highest in all of the above.

Even more surprising was a 2010 Wayne State University research project that examined the photos of major league players on baseball cards issued in 1952. Researchers assessed emotions by smile intensity based on the premise that the authenticity of your grin conveys the depth of your positive emotions. The cards were divided into unsmiling, partial smile, and big smile. The study found that the span of a player's smile could actually predict *longevity*! Players who didn't smile in their pictures lived an average of only 72.9 years, partial smilers averaged 75 years, and players with beaming smiles lived an average of 79.9 years.[6]

So there you have it. If you want to add years to your life, just smile and laugh. The grace suggestion for this chapter may be the most pleasant one so far. It requires no personal introspection, painful forgiveness, or disciplined denial. I cheerfully offer a win-win-win-win idea.

Just laugh.

And take extra joy in the knowledge that fifteen minutes of laughter burns up to forty calories.[7]

There is a wonderful proverb that fits well here: "If you are too busy to laugh, you are too busy."

Laugh it up and share this gift with others. And if I might paraphrase a familiar Sunday school song . . .

If you're happy and you know it,
Tell your face.
If you're happy and you know it,
Tell your face.
If you're happy and you know it,
Then it seems your face should show it.
If you're happy and you know it,
Tell your face.

Will you join me in promoting a grassroots revival of mirth and merriment? Get out there and laugh!

GOD'S TAKE

Those who listen to instruction will prosper;
those who trust the LORD will be joyful.

PROVERBS 16:20

A DOSE OF GRACE

*Laugh. Schedule a minimum of fifteen minutes
with whatever makes you laugh. Go to a comedy
club, watch a funny YouTube video (I love dog
ones), read a humorous story or book, or rent a
movie. Preferably, share the laughter with others,
because glee in the company of friends increases
the benefits. Comedian Milton Berle quipped that
"laughter is an instant vacation." Book it every day.
This simple exercise will improve your heart health,
memory, immune system, disposition, and longevity.
You're welcome!*

CHAPTER 15

WE NEED A VILLAGE

Christ distributes courage through community; he dissipates doubts through fellowship. He never deposits all knowledge in one person but distributes pieces of the jigsaw puzzle to many. When you interlock your understanding with mine, and we share our discoveries, when we mix, mingle, confess and pray, Christ speaks.

MAX LUCADO[1]

DURING OUR HILL COUNTRY GETAWAY, the "ducks were on the pond." Baseball fans will recognize that phrase as a colorful way to describe having a runner on every base. But this time I was enjoying some time off from the baseball gig with my lovely bride, and the ducks were literally on the pond. We were sitting on the porch of our little cabin near Fredericksburg, Texas, when a flock of seven mallards noisily left the pond and waddled toward us on bright orange legs and webbed feet. The distinctive green heads of the two male ducks shimmered, accented by white neck rings.

They lined up and quacked expectantly. This was not their first tourist-manipulating rodeo. If I spoke duck, I suspect the translation would have been something like the famous line from *Caddyshack*: "Hey, how about a little something, you know, for the effort, you know." Our offering of cereal flakes apparently was acceptable.

Every time we went out on our porch, the ducks would make a beeline, er, duckline for us and wait for their snack. Joni and I were fascinated by their behavior. The five female and two male ducks always stayed together.

There was a clear leader of the team, and when the leader decided it was time to move on to other activities, the other six dutifully followed. They swam at the same time. Groomed at the same time. Slept at the same time.

When the ducks lined up for nap time, Joni and I noticed something else odd. The ducks at the end of the line had one eye closed and one open. The other ducks closed both eyes and rested. During our visit they took turns sharing this responsibility.

I found out that the ducks at the end of the line can control which side of the brain is awake and which snoozes. The fancy name is single-hemisphere sleep. The eye connected to the side of the brain that was sleeping was closed, while the awake side kept watch for the group. What an amazing skill to possess! How great would that be for boring meetings? But I digress.

The other ducks felt safe to sleep with lookouts in place. And the ducks on duty at least got some rest while still protecting the others.

We loved watching our mallard friends for a few days. Clearly they were created to thrive in community. The truth is, so are we.

Community is a basic human need. Howard Schultz, Starbucks chairman and CEO, saw that need. According to the company website, when he joined Starbucks, he wanted to create a place for human connection, conversation, and one that fostered a sense of community—a third place between work and home.[2] That was the genesis of one of the most successful business models in history.

One of the places that used to be the third place between work and home was the church. For many, it still is the community that matters, but for many more, church is a place to be avoided at all costs. I talked to a Christian leader on a college campus in Texas, and he relayed the challenge of engaging students in spiritual discussions. One primary issue is getting young men and women to attend the Christian events. "We have to make sure that they don't think it is church."

What happened? Why is church a repellent to young people? My generation shares some of the blame. We talked but did not model faith to our kids. The church also shares some of the blame for not aggressively proclaiming the scandalous nature of grace. We allowed an image of "holier than thou" and the proclamation of what we are against to be the face of the church. We talked about the repulsiveness of sin instead of the forgiveness of sin.

We have somehow proffered the narrative that church requires individuals to undergo a begrudging moral cleanup in order to be worthy of inclusion in the club. The attractiveness of the church should be that you don't have to shape up, you don't have to clean up, and your sin is your admission ticket to the room of grace and forgiveness.

Why do so many people prefer the coffeehouse over the church house? Why is the local bar often a more welcoming place of acceptance than the church? I used to write a blog about any song that happened to cycle up when I hit shuffle on my iPod. It was a dangerous challenge.

One day the song that came up was "I Love This Bar"

by Toby Keith. He sings how every time he walks into that gathering, it puts a big smile on his face. There are all kinds of colorful people there—winners, losers, chain smokers, boozers, bikers, yuppies, and maybe even a hooker. Sounds exactly like the crowd that got Jesus in trouble with religious types of His day.

> By this time a lot of men and women of doubtful reputation were hanging around Jesus, listening intently. The Pharisees and religion scholars were not pleased, not at all pleased. They growled, "He takes in sinners and eats meals with them, treating them like old friends."
>
> LUKE 15:1-2, MSG

Jesus obviously was comfortable with being in the company of people who were not so self-righteous that they refused to examine their hearts. The dynamic that Luke recorded compelled author Philip Yancey to write,

> Having spent time around "sinners" and also around purported saints, I have a hunch why Jesus spent so much time with the former group: I think he preferred their company. Because the sinners were honest about themselves and had no pretense, Jesus could deal with them. In contrast, the saints put on airs, judged him, and sought to catch him in a moral trap. In the end it was the saints, not the sinners, who arrested Jesus.[3]

In the end it is the saints, and not the sinners, who have perverted the hope of the gospel.

All of us want a place where we are accepted as is. That is the appeal of the neighborhood bar or the local over-priced coffeehouse. We are designed for community, and the church needs to realize that it must be a place of teaching and reproach but, perhaps more importantly, a place of refuge, grace, and safety. A walk-in clinic for messy Christians and messy seekers. The truth is that all of us are messy. If most people honestly relayed the condition of their souls, as soon as they walked in the door, they would be triaged with a code blue of love, concern, and hope.

With the endless availability of teaching materials, books, podcasts, and other resources, American Christians don't lack for instruction. What we seem to be missing is the community of love and acceptance that ignited the early church. A place where you can come as you are and experience grace. That is the church I dream about.

That is the church that rocked the world in the first century after Jesus' Ascension. The writer of Hebrews encourages me to lean fully into God's love, and from that base I can love others.

> So let's *do* it—full of belief, confident that we're presentable inside and out. Let's keep a firm grip on the promises that keep us going. He always keeps his word. Let's see how inventive we can be in encouraging love and helping out, not avoiding worshiping together as some do but spurring each other on, especially as we see the big Day approaching.
>
> HEBREWS 10:22-25, MSG

Clearly we are called to worship together and to be an encouragement to one another. At our home church,

Waterbrook Bible Fellowship in Wylie, Texas, we have small community groups that we call "home teams." Joni and I share life together in complete honesty with twelve other folks from our church. When a need comes up, the prayer request goes out, and the response is an encouragement every time. The e-mail thread lights up with multiple comments like "praying" and "on it." Recently, when I had minor surgery, lead pastor Jeff Denton asked me why I hadn't let him know so he could pray.

"My home team was on it," I said. "No need to bother you when that support group is around me."

That is how it should work in community. Not all of us have experienced the joy of Psalm 133:1: "Behold, how good and pleasant it is when brothers dwell in unity!" (ESV).

There is no more powerful community than a group of believers who live in unity. And nothing should level the playing field like embracing the teachings of Jesus. He cares not a whit about color, status, or appearance. Jesus looks only on the heart.

In Paul's letter to the Thessalonians, he offered the benefits of honest community:

> Brothers and sisters, we urge you to warn those who are lazy. Encourage those who are timid. Take tender care of those who are weak. Be patient with everyone.
>
> I THESSALONIANS 5:14

Isn't it interesting that the challenges Paul lists are arranged from easiest to hardest? I can admonish the lazy all day long. I am pretty good about encouraging the timid. On my good days I help the weak. But be patient with them all? Come on, Paul. Do you know these people?

But that is the attraction of community. It is messy and beautiful. Frustrating and fulfilling. It is life. And it is best lived together with other messy, beautiful, frustrating, and fulfilling saints who still are quite capable of sinning.

And that tees up the biggest need for community as found in Galatians:

> Dear brothers and sisters, if another believer is overcome by some sin, you who are godly should **gently and humbly help that person back onto the right path.** And be careful not to fall into the same temptation yourself. **Share each other's burdens, and in this way obey the law of Christ. If you think you are too important to help someone, you are only fooling yourself. You are not that important.**
>
> GALATIANS 6:1-3 (EMPHASIS ADDED)

That seems like such an essential passage for this culture as I contemplate the devastating and heartbreaking toll of sin. I know. That is not politically correct. But there is no other word that describes what I am seeing today. Since I began this project, I have seen a beloved and effective pastor lose his ministry for the false hope of an inappropriate relationship. Somehow he stepped away from the power of grace in community and listened to the siren song of sin.

Sin says that there is more. Sin says that you deserve to be happier and that it will be true only in a different relationship. Sin says that God does not really have your best interest at heart. I hate those lies from Satan that we continue to believe.

People are desperate to find community and a sense of belonging, and they often find it in the wrong places. I see precious men and women (sometimes boys and girls) lose their lives because they found identity in groups that promised family and acceptance but delivered heartbreak and death. These souls likely had found that dynamic of acceptance nowhere else in their experience. All of us want to find someone who will accept us for who we are. These lonely souls found identity in a group that provided acceptance but not safety.

Lest I jump to judgment (as I am so skilled at doing), I should wonder instead what led this pastor to leave his first love, and what leads men and women to pursue a group that would ultimately lead to violence, crime, and death.

I am sad that we have too often failed to create a community that does not flinch at inappropriate language, clothing, and behavior. Do you think Jesus would look at a tattoo or at the heart? Would He hear the ugly words of a hurting person or the desperate tone of his need? Would He condemn the sin or embrace the sinner and whisper gently in her ear that there is a better way? Of course, there are consequences to sin, made ever more clear when we turn on the news every day. But the truth is that all of us are sinners.

My primary career is in television and will continue to be until more of you buy my books! Live television is a high-energy world of edgy emotions, fast-paced decisions, and honest language. It is not always a safe place for the easily offended. But it is an honest place with real people willing to hear your story when you don't step back in self-righteous offense.

For years I looked outside this community to find a meaningful place to serve God. I volunteered at other ministries. I prayed for God to show me what I could do. Finally, I realized the obvious—my ministry was all around me. Not in pushy agendas to people intimidated by my position. My role is responding with love to the needs of people whom I live life with every day and who know my heart. People like my friend Mike, whom you met at the beginning of this book.

I simply walked with him when he was struggling. He was open because I had a relationship of trust in place with him. I suspect many, if not most, followers of Jesus have similar opportunities to love those around them. You have to be present and connected to their lives. And maybe disconnected from devices long enough to talk to them and find out what is going on in their lives.

Christians really do have a wonderful message of hope. But too often we don't communicate the liberating joy of the gospel. We attach strings, instead of shouting that all we need to bring to Him for salvation is our sin and need. Jesus has done the rest.

Paul makes it pretty simple:

> If you openly declare that Jesus is Lord and believe in your heart that God raised him from the dead, you will be saved.
>
> ROMANS 10:9

I must begin to concentrate on the message of what Jesus has done for me. Whether my sin inventory fills multiple volumes or a Post-it note is irrelevant. I need the Cross. Only the finished work of Jesus makes me flawless. I am wounded and need acceptance. My heart grieves for that pastor and his family. I ache for souls lost to gang violence. The former forgot the power of the gospel, and most likely, the latter never heard or almost certainly never witnessed its unconditional love and liberating power. Lord, forgive me for my sinful judgment of wounded souls, and help me to be a light to a very dark world.

At Boys Town outside Omaha, Nebraska, there is a statue of a young boy carrying a smaller boy on his back. The inscription reads, "He ain't heavy, Father . . . he's m' brother," which is the answer a priest received when he asked if the young man needed help with his burden.[4]

And yes, those words became the inspiration for a song written by Bobby Scott and Bob Russell that became a hit for the Hollies in 1969. That slogan is what real community should look like in the church. I understand why so many Christians are reluctant to jump into unvarnished and honest relationship with other believers. Immersing yourself in the lives of others is messy, sad, and difficult. And in a great paradox of our faith, it is the most fulfilling thing you can do.

I have taken the risk of trusting a group of men with everything that is true about me, and they have done the same with me. That commitment to trust these men with my weaknesses has been one of the best things I have ever done to grow in my faith. We have shared triumphs and tragedy. Hilarity and heartbreak. We have confessed our fears and exposed our shame to the healing power of relationship in the light of the Holy Spirit.

Putting all of your cards on the relationship table is a scary play. But when you play all your cards and you are still loved, it is the most exhilarating and freeing thing you can imagine. I shared with these men my long pattern of passive-aggressive reactions to Joni. They counseled me, prayed with me, encouraged me, and then they called Joni and shared what they had told me. They asked her to be honest with them if I fell back on that behavior. I have rarely heard her at such a loss for words as she was at such a bold and caring commitment from these men.

That is the beauty of Christian community. That is how

it should work. That is what Paul was writing about to the church in Galatia when he instructed them to "share" one another's burdens.

Sometimes I have been the one who has been strong and had the privilege of carrying my brother. The miracle of grace is that it never breaks us to share a brother's burden. I will confess that part of my learning process has been to allow others to be strong for me. I love to help others, but I often choose to not bother others with my trials. That ain't how this journey works. I deny others the privilege of serving when I foolishly try to be self-sufficient. My pride short-circuits the healing ministry of grace in community.

We need each other. God created that longing in our hearts to be in community. I pray that we will have the courage to honestly live that way.

GOD'S TAKE

I appeal to you, dear brothers and sisters, by the authority of our Lord Jesus Christ, to live in harmony with each other. Let there be no divisions in the church. Rather, be of one mind, united in thought and purpose.

1 CORINTHIANS 1:10

A DOSE OF GRACE

I am grateful that Scripture recognizes our need for one another on this journey. Share your journey with your brothers and sisters in Christian community. I know that some have tried and been wounded. Some have tried and been ignored. I have been there too. I encourage you (make that plead with you) to not give up. Pray for those connections. Maybe you need to be the one who takes the risk to start building a room of grace where other brothers and sisters can come to find healing. This isn't easy. Worthwhile endeavors rarely are.

CHAPTER 16

THE DOUBT BOUT

*In faith there is enough light for those who want to believe
and enough shadows to blind those who don't.*

BLAISE PASCAL

THE WORDS FROM MY WIFE hit me like a punch in the gut.

"If I'm going to be by myself anyway, I'm not sure I want to be married."

That devastating and emotional moment came as a culmination of many years of my hard-driving work, travel, and self-absorption. Like many men, I did not realize the full extent of how much I had dumped on Joni until that moment. I had never experienced doubt like I felt at that moment. I was unsure if my marriage would survive. I was frightened about my relationship with my boys. I felt I had betrayed my faith.

Joni was dealing with three rambunctious young boys, and much of the time doing it by herself. When I was home, I tried to be a good dad and be with my sons. The person left out was Joni.

I got the message. I recognized what I had done. I asked for forgiveness, and Joni graciously gave it. I began the process of rebuilding our marriage and Joni's trust. We went to work on our relationship, and by the grace of God, we were able to restore our marriage through hard work and changes that I willingly made.

Life together was good again. After several years of growing together, we were approaching the empty nest with anticipation of travel and more freedom. We were truly happy.

And then in 2006 we both got punched in the gut. Joni called with the news from her doctor's report and could hardly get out one sentence.

"My biopsy is cancer."

I watched her look cancer in the eye and not blink. We had confidence in our doctors. We had confidence in our God and His plan for our lives. But there is something about the devastating impact of the word *cancer* that causes doubts to churn like storm-tossed surf.

The first chemotherapy session was a difficult day for both of us. The doctors had explained the strategy. We would hit the cancer hard and aggressively because Joni was young, strong, and determined. I remember Dr. Archana Ganaraj looking at Joni and saying, "Give me one year, and I will give you the rest of your life."

It was a powerful and helpful promise. But we still fought doubt about the terrible cost of cancer treatment. Joni would face a year of chemotherapy, radiation, and additional infusion therapy with a drug that could arrest her cancer but could also damage her heart. This was going to be a marathon of emotional, physical, and spiritual ups and downs.

The reality settled over us in late April of that year as I watched toxic chemicals drip, drip, drip into my wife's bloodstream. We were trusting our doctor's recommendation of putting poison into Joni's veins to kill the fast-growing cancer cells. One of Joni's chemo drugs included a derivative of rat poison. This combination of drugs is called cocktail chemotherapy, and the "mixed drink" is aptly nicknamed the "red devil."

You have to have a lot of faith in your doctors to allow them to hook you up to chemicals that are on a mission to hunt down and destroy fast-growing cells. But there is a catch. The "red devil" can't discriminate between good and bad cells, which meant Joni would lose her hair, since good hair-follicle cells grow quickly.

The wonderful news is that we just celebrated ten years of cancer-free time together. But I can still remember the fear in the initial diagnosis and the doubt we had to face. There was plenty of evidence that Joni would be okay. And, thanks to the Internet, lots of evidence that this could end badly. We had to proceed in faith together, and we did.

Those memories resurfaced when I started thinking and writing about doubt as a follower of Jesus. I'm sure you know by now that I am not a "professional" Christian. I am not a theologian or a preacher. I am not a philosopher or an apologist. I am a man trying to live my life well, in relationship with my God, my wife, my family, my friends, and my community. I also live that quest mostly outside the Christian bubble that can provide cover and comfort.

In the secular world I work in, some may respect me personally but think my faith convictions are antiquated, absurd, and maybe dangerous. They hear the unbiblical and outrageous claims of some fringe groups and perhaps wonder if I share any of those beliefs. I have friends and family who love me but think I am a little whacked to believe that a man claimed to be God, got Himself killed, and then rose from the dead. They cannot comprehend how I could base my life on such a story. Sometimes their questioning gives me pause and troubles my soul. Some of these questioners are really smart people. I have never been that guy who can just bluster my way past those who have honest disagreements. Too often, I have seen that absolute certainty is the trump card of a fool.

Today I come completely clean in my journey to live more in the moment. I still wrestle with doubt. Yet, honestly, I don't face the dark-depression doubt that some suffer. Mine is more of a "what if at the end of this life I find that the beliefs I based my life on are not true?" kind of doubt.

Many have doubts because they were "born into" faith and never really examined it for themselves. That was not my story. My family did not indoctrinate me. We went to a little church near our home only on Christmas and Easter. My family was not agnostic; we just didn't talk about God a lot. My sister, Sherry, came to faith, and I followed her to church as a young teen. I started my faith journey in a church that espoused the bumper sticker theology of "God says it, I believe it, that settles it." That failure to address doubts creates a faith that is fragile and easily destroyed. Philip Yancey shares a similar faith, beginning as mine did, and it is probably not surprising that he has endured seasons of doubt. He offered this intriguing take during an interview:

> When I speak to college students, I challenge them to find a single argument against God in the older agnostics (Bertrand Russell, Voltaire, David Hume) or the newer ones (Richard Dawkins, Christopher Hitchens, Sam Harris) that is not already included

in books like Psalms, Job, Habakkuk, and
Lamentations. I have respect for a God who not only
gives us the freedom to reject him, but also includes
the arguments we can use in the Bible. God seems
rather doubt-tolerant, actually.[1]

That is the truth. The Bible is pretty open with honest
doubters. So why is this topic not discussed more openly in
our faith community? I mentioned earlier that I am writing this book during the political season. What a great time
to disconnect from devices! I realized that even more after
watching a couple of the debates on television. I see a parallel to our faith in the spokespeople for each candidate.
After each debate, they have a "spin room" where apologists
explain why their candidate won the night, and they rationalize why something the candidate said that was clearly
wrong really wasn't wrong at all. What a strange job. Yet I
tend to do the same thing with my faith. Instead of own-
ing my sin and doubt, I am tempted to "spin" my sin with
bumper sticker excuses. "I am sorry that I hurt you, please
forgive me" is much more powerful than "I'm not perfect,
just forgiven."

So I am not going to spin my doubt. I am going to be
honest about my journey and conclusion. I agree with Pastor
Tim Keller's analogy.

A faith without some doubts is like a human body
with no antibodies in it. People who blithely go
through life too busy or indifferent to ask the
hard questions about why they believe as they do
will find themselves defenseless against either the
experience of tragedy or the probing questions

of a smart skeptic. A person's faith can collapse almost overnight if she failed over the years to listen patiently to her own doubts, which should only be discarded after long reflection.[2]

Time magazine ranked the most important historical figures by combining millions of traces of opinions and then analyzing that data to create individual values and rankings, much like Google ranks web pages. Number one on the list was Jesus Christ.[3]

I am fascinated by the impact of this man. From the time Jesus began His three-year ministry, He never had an office or residence. When a person tagging along with the Nazarene asked to join the group, Jesus gave fair warning. "Foxes have dens to live in, and birds have nests, but the Son of Man has no place even to lay his head" (Luke 9:58).

Singer-songwriter Rich Mullins wrote that "the hope of the whole world rests on the shoulders of a homeless man."[4] Jesus came from a family of modest means. He was brought up on the wrong side of the culturally acceptable tracks in the town of Nazareth. Jesus was beginning to assemble the group of men that would become known as the apostles. Philip was one of the new followers, and he enthusiastically informed his friend Nathanael about his new calling. Nathanael's first reaction was doubt.

> "We have found the very person Moses and the prophets wrote about! His name is Jesus, the son of Joseph from Nazareth."
>
> "Nazareth!" exclaimed Nathanael. "Can anything good come from Nazareth?"
>
> JOHN 1:45-46

Nathanael's question about anything good coming out of Nazareth was a remarkable query. Putting it in the context of my Ohio roots, that would be like asking, "Can anything good come out of Ann Arbor?" Jesus did not recruit a single person of "power" to further His campaign. He did not write a book. He did not speak at influential venues. Jesus did not lobby a single political leader. He did not try to glad-hand the religious leaders to support His mission. He never used any kind of force or coercion. If Jesus encountered resistance, He picked up and moved on.

Jesus simply walked, talked, taught, healed, loved, and invested in the lives of twelve very ordinary men. From that résumé came a faith community that numbers more than two billion people today. The group that was dubbed "Christians" continued to expand in spite of the indefensible things that have been done under the guise of His name. I have often said that one of the greatest apologetics for the Christian faith is that it continues to flourish in spite of Christians!

Jesus' claims were mind boggling. Jesus said that He was God in human flesh. Buddha never claimed to be God. He said, "I am a teacher in search of the truth." Mohammed never claimed to be God. Mohammed said, "Unless God throws his cloak of mercy over me, I have no hope." Confucius never claimed to be God. Confucius said, "I never claimed to be holy." Yet Jesus Christ claimed to be the true and living God. Jesus said, "I am the way, the truth, and the life" (John 14:6).[5] Once you look closely at what each person claimed, how can you honestly say that all religions are the same? C. S. Lewis famously summed it up:

A man who was merely a man and said the sort of things Jesus said would not be a great moral teacher.

He would either be a lunatic—on a level with the
man who says he is a poached egg—or else he would
be the Devil of Hell. You must make your choice.
Either this man was, and is, the Son of God; or else
a madman or something worse. You can shut Him
up for a fool, you can spit at Him and kill him as a
demon; or you can fall at His feet and call Him Lord
and God. But let us not come with any patronizing
nonsense about His being a great human teacher. He
has not left that open to us. He did not intend to.[6]

That was why the story line of the movie *Risen* was intriguing to me. Historically, there was a Nazarene who was cruci-
fied, and two groups had a tremendous interest in making sure
that his death was the end of the story. The Romans wanted
no movement to grow so large that it would cause political
unrest. The Jewish leaders wanted to stamp out the heresy that
they believed this Teacher was spreading, in order to keep their
power intact. It was a win-win situation for the religious leaders and Rome to eliminate this messianic hope of the people.

The story is told through the eyes of a Roman military
tribune named Clavius tasked by Pilate to make sure Jesus'
crazy followers did not steal the body. This was *not* a grace
suggestion from Pilate! A story had been circulating that the
Nazarene would rise again in three days, so Clavius made
sure the massive stone was rolled into place over the entrance
to the tomb and sealed. Roman soldiers guarded the tomb,
knowing full well they could be killed if they failed to keep
the body secured.

Three days later the body was gone, and Clavius began a
desperate hunt. The battle-hardened soldier could not accept
that this Nazarene named Jesus could have somehow come

back to life. That is a step of faith that people are still wrestling with two thousand years later. But it is the most important question of all, if you are to put your faith in Jesus.

If Jesus did not rise from the dead, then there really is no difference in this man and any other great moral teacher. But if Jesus did rise from the dead, then His words are different from the words of any other teacher. All of Christianity depends on what happened in that event.

Risen explores the imagined lengths that the Romans and religious leaders went to in order to quell the rumor that Jesus had risen. They tried to find the body (or any similar body that might pass for his) that could be displayed to stop the rumors. They were not successful.

I struggled with these same questions forty-something years ago:

- How could the body disappear?
- How did a bunch of cowards like the apostles become heroes of the faith and become willing to die martyrs' deaths? Simply because they stole the body out of a tomb?
- Could they have kept a lie of such massive implications secret?

I love the way former Watergate principal Chuck Colson honestly evaluated the event:

I know the resurrection is a fact, and Watergate proved it to me. How? Because 12 men testified they had seen Jesus raised from the dead, then they proclaimed that truth for 40 years, never once denying it. Everyone was beaten, tortured, stoned and put in prison.

They would not have endured that if it weren't true. Watergate embroiled 12 of the most powerful men in the world—and they couldn't keep a lie for three weeks. You're telling me 12 apostles could keep a lie for 40 years? Absolutely impossible.

Honest people can view the same evidence and come up with completely different opinions. I wrestled with the claims of Jesus Christ for a long time before I decided to believe that He was who He claimed to be. And I remember feeling exactly what the fictional character Clavius felt when he was asked what he feared most: "Being wrong. Wagering eternity on it."

I have never been able to accept the idea that there is no design or purpose to this life. People who do not accept faith think that humankind naturally evolved into doing the right things in community for the common good. I believe something or Someone writes that on our hearts. I see creative genius that I cannot account for as accidental.

Perhaps the most important argument for me is the impact that the Nazarene teacher has had on my life. I have haphazardly attempted to follow Him for many years. Tolstoy's quote fittingly describes my awkward attempts: "If I know the way home and am walking along it drunkenly, is it any less the right way because I am staggering from side to side!"

I used to have a difficult time being wrong. My lack of self-confidence as a college dropout caused me to react really negatively if someone or something made me feel dumb. I would defend indefensible positions or actions rather than admit that I was wrong. As I grew in my relationship with and understanding of Jesus, I began to slowly redefine my identity. My worth is not in always being right or being the smartest guy in the room. My worth is defined by being a child of God and a friend of Jesus. When I keep my eyes on Jesus, I maintain a better perspective on every area of my life.

The apostles followed Jesus and saw that it was not an easy choice at times. Many followers were deserting Jesus after some difficult teaching.

> At this point many of his disciples turned away and deserted him. Then Jesus turned to the Twelve and asked, "Are you also going to leave?"
>
> Simon Peter replied, "Lord, to whom would we go? You have the words that give eternal life. We believe, and we know you are the Holy One of God."
> JOHN 6:66-69

That is my belief. I am drawn to Jesus. I believe that God decided to redeem man through this outlandish plan. No religion offers redemption without works other than the gospel of Jesus. I believe I have seen His hand over and over in my life. But if I am wrong and had the opportunity to live my life over again, I can honestly say I would change nothing.

I consider a life pursuing the impossible goal of becoming like Jesus to be more valuable than any honor or possession I could attain. The teachings of Jesus are so amazing and so radical that I cannot imagine that any man could have imagined them. If you drill down into just His words, you will find a sacred pathway that is worth seeking.

I believe my marriage is still intact because I have followed the teachings of Jesus. I don't say that lightly. I honestly believe that without that faith commitment, Joni and I would not have survived. Whatever kind things that my friends and colleagues might say about me are in large part due to how I believe I should respond to them based on the words of Christ. I have been shaped and matured by this radical Rabbi who changed history. He changed me.

Tim Keller puts it this way:

> The Christian Gospel is that I am so flawed that Jesus had to die for me, yet I am so loved and valued that Jesus was glad to die for me. This leads to deep humility and deep confidence at the same time. It undermines both swaggering and sniveling. I cannot feel superior to anyone, and yet I have nothing to prove to anyone. I do not think more of myself nor less of myself. Instead, I think of myself less.[7]

I have been changed by these truths. I have confronted my doubts and I have chosen to stay focused on the claims of this Rabbi from Nazareth. If I am wagering my eternity, I choose to wager on Jesus.

GOD'S TAKE

You must show mercy to those whose faith is wavering.

JUDE 1:22

A DOSE OF GRACE

Doubt is not a sign of weakness but a sign of strength. Don't run from your doubt. Confront your doubt with study, quiet reflection, prayer, and conversation with fellow believers. You will emerge stronger and deeper in your faith by confronting your doubt instead of blindly hoping.

CHAPTER 17

POWERED BY PRAYER

Prayer is simply a two-way conversation between you and God.

BILLY GRAHAM

ONE OF MY GREAT SPIRITUAL EPIPHANIES came while listening to a Garth Brooks song. I know. But at this point, what did you expect? The song is called "Unanswered Prayers," and Garth sings about things that he fervently begged for God to provide. Now, years later, he can see how much better things are because those prayers were unanswered. I have shared the same experience many times. I would suggest that unanswered is an answer, but I guess that would not make a catchy lyric.

I remember praying for a particular job that would give me prestige and allow me to climb the ladder in the broadcast world. It looked like the offer was about to come, and then it did not. I was disappointed. Confused. *What happened?*

In retrospect, I believe that God moved in that situation

and firmly slammed the door shut. I can see now that it was not even close to being a good fit for me. It was a high-pressure position where performance was often more important than people. Instead, God put me in a place where my relational gifts could be used to not only direct good sports telecasts but also to invest in the lives of those I work with every day. Today I thank God that He said no to my prayer.

I remember hearing a wonderful story about a prayer that was spoken in a little country church.

> The new pastor called on one of his older deacons to lead in the opening prayer. The deacon stood up, bowed his head and said, "Lord, I hate buttermilk."
>
> The pastor opened one eye and wondered where this was going. The deacon continued, "Lord, I hate lard." Now the pastor was totally perplexed. The deacon continued, "Lord, I ain't too crazy about plain flour. But after you mix 'em all together and bake 'em in a hot oven, I just love biscuits.
>
> "Lord, help us to realize when life gets hard, when things come up that we don't like, whenever we don't understand what You are doing, that we need to wait and see what You are making. After you get through mixing and baking, it'll probably be something even better than biscuits. Amen."[1]

We make prayer so complex and hard. Philip Yancey wrote that "most of the great books on prayer are written by 'experts'—monks, missionaries, mystics, saints. I've read scores of them, and mainly they make me feel guilty."[2]

If I may quote from the wisdom of Curly of the Three

Stooges, "I resemble that remark." I have way overthought and overstressed prayer. I hear people talking about how they pray for hours and hours. And I feel more like the disciples who fell asleep in the garden than like a prayer warrior.

> He returned to the disciples and found them asleep. He said to Peter, "Couldn't you watch with me even one hour? Keep watch and pray, so that you will not give in to temptation. For the spirit is willing, but the body is weak!"
> MATTHEW 26:40-41

That has been my refrain for too many years. The spirit is willing, but the body is weak. I have struggled with my attention deficit as a real, and sometimes convenient, excuse for my prayer difficulties.

Prayer is paramount to my relationship with God. If I am going to be more present and more connected to God, it is critical that I understand the power of prayer. In keeping with my orthodox approach to spiritual growth, I turned to football for insight into the importance of fundamentals.

I love football. The opening of football training camps gets my juices going. I watch some of the greatest athletes in the world getting ready to play a highly skilled game. So what do they start with every summer at training camp?

Footwork and technique drills. Coaches demanding constant repetition of essential skills. The best teams are the ones that consistently execute the most basic fundamental aspects of their craft.

Legendary Green Bay Packers coach Vince Lombardi famously began each training camp by gathering wide-eyed rookies and grizzled veterans around him. Holding the pigskin in front of him, he would solemnly proclaim an indisputable truth.

"Gentlemen, this is a football."

From that rather rudimentary start he would detail the importance of understanding the foundations of the sport. I can learn something from that approach. When I first came to faith, I was so excited to learn the requisite skills of faith. How do I study the Bible? How do I pray? How do I grow in my faith? But something seemed to happen as I accumulated some seasons under my belt.

I forgot the fundamentals. I started looking for the latest trend in faith. Which trendy Christian leader should I emulate next? I defined myself by movements, instead of by Jesus, the Cross, and His finished work. For me, football training camp is another reminder that I desperately need the indispensable basics of faith.

Fundamentals are best taught by those who have the gift of teaching and complete knowledge of the skills required. You hope you can find an expert to teach you. That is exactly why the disciples came to Jesus and asked for His help on how to pray. They had watched Him pray. They knew how important prayer was to Jesus. Now they asked Him to teach them. Here is Luke's "pray-by-pray" of that moment:

> One day Jesus was praying in a certain place. When he finished, one of his disciples said to him, "Lord, teach us to pray, just as John taught his disciples."
> He said to them, "When you pray, say:
> 'Father,
> hallowed be your name,
> your kingdom come.
> Give us each day our daily bread.

Forgive us our sins,
>   for we also forgive everyone who sins against us.
And lead us not into temptation.'"

LUKE 11:1-4, NIV

Over much of my fumbling, bumbling Christian journey, I would skip straight to the "give us our daily bread and forgive us our sins" parts of that prayer. I managed to miss the most important foundational aspect of this insightful prayer. The first fundamental is contained in the opening word.

Father.

I get to relate to God as my Father! That privilege comes only from my relationship with Jesus. Noted preacher Haddon Robinson stated that in the entire Old Testament, God is called Father only seven times, and it is always in respect to the nation of Israel. There is never a recorded instance where any individual dared to address the Sovereign God as Father.

Now Jesus comes on the scene, and Robinson writes about the amazing contrast:

> Yet in the New Testament, at least 275 times, that is how we are instructed to speak to God. Because of Jesus's death and resurrection, when we come to the sovereign majesty of the universe the word that should fall readily from our lips is *Father.*[3]

That is a game changer! I can come to the God of the universe, who knows my sin, my weakness, and my failure, and call Him Father! Are you kidding me?

I also tended to zoom by the next essential teaching.

Hallowed be your name.

Prayer starts not with a shopping list of what I need God

to do, but instead with worship and recognition of *who God is*. We are coached by Jesus to remember how great God is and to recognize that His ways are not our ways. We are taught to remember that His holiness is perfect, and His grace is our hope. Hallowed be Your name.

When I learn those fundamentals, the rest of the offense falls into place. He is my Father who loves me and wants the best for me. He hears me, and He responds. If the answer is no, that is an answer. That may mean my request will be answered later. It may be answered differently. It may not be answered at all. But through all of those responses, I trust that He is holy, powerful, and present.

As has been the pattern in this journey, I decided to check the Owner's Manual for instruction on more basics of prayer:

> Always be joyful. Never stop praying. Be thankful in all circumstances, for this is God's will for you who belong to Christ Jesus.
>
> I THESSALONIANS 5:16-18

> Don't worry about anything; instead, pray about everything. Tell God what you need, and thank him for all he has done.
>
> PHILIPPIANS 4:6

> Rejoice in our confident hope. Be patient in trouble, and keep on praying.
>
> ROMANS 12:12

I struggled also with the idea of being in constant prayer. I used to view prayer as a "stop everything and focus completely on God" activity. I would compare myself to those

who claimed to pray for hours a day. But if that were the pro-
tocol, Paul's words to the church at Thessalonica would make
no sense. If I stopped everything to pray but never stopped
praying, I would never accomplish anything! I would truly
be so heavenly minded that I would be of no earthly good.

I learned an important principle from the story of
Nehemiah. He was the cup bearer to King Artaxerxes. We
think of a cup bearer as the poor soul who makes sure the
king's food and wine is not poisoned, but this influential
position encompassed more than that. Nehemiah would be
akin to a modern-day executive assistant who has the ear and
trust of a powerful CEO. He was surrounded by luxury. This
was a good gig, but it depended on his staying in the good
graces of the king.

One day Nehemiah heard about the terrible condition of
Jerusalem's wall from his brother Hanani and other men who
had recently returned from the city. The report devastated
Nehemiah, and he wept, mourned, fasted, and prayed for
days. God gave him a desire to rebuild the wall, but he needed
the blessing of the king to be released to his mission. This was
not a simple HR request. If the king was angered, Nehemiah
could be punished or even killed. But in Nehemiah's story,
there is a great insight into how you can "pray" constantly
when you are in relationship with God.

Nehemiah had his moment before the king. He felt compelled by God to follow his heart, a clue to what being in
constant prayer looks like.

Some translations say Nehemiah was afraid or terrified as
he appealed to the king. What he did is a lesson for all of us.

The king asked, "Well, how can I help you?"
With a prayer to the God of heaven, I replied, "If

it please the king, and if you are pleased with me, your servant, send me to Judah to rebuild the city where my ancestors are buried."

The king, with the queen sitting beside him, asked, "How long will you be gone? When will you return?" After I told him how long I would be gone, the king agreed to my request.

NEHEMIAH 2:4-6

I think *The Message* captures the moment best.

Praying under my breath to the God-of-Heaven, I said, "If it please the king, and if the king thinks well of me, send me to Judah, to the city where my family is buried, so that I can rebuild it." (verses 4-5)

Praying does not need to be solemn, on-your-knees petitioning. It can be simply aligning your thoughts and heart to God. It is being in consistent awareness of His majesty, holiness, love, and grace. Remember the starting premise of this book? God knows our very thoughts, as described in Psalm 139.

Prayer gives us a chance to acknowledge God and order our will with His. So praying constantly is actually a very doable thing. It can be a simple thought with an under-your-breath petition to God, who already knows your heart and thoughts. And I suppose I should remind myself again that the device might need to be unplugged in order to be plugged in to God in prayer.

Jesus stated an interesting truth right before His instructions on how we should pray.

When you pray, don't babble on and on as the Gentiles do. They think their prayers are answered merely by repeating their words again and again. Don't be like them, for **your Father knows exactly what you need even before you ask him!**

MATTHEW 6:7-8 (EMPHASIS ADDED)

So why even go through the effort if He knows already? Because it creates relationship with God. Jesus obviously did not mean to indicate that prayer is not vital. Look at His own example!

Whenever Jesus faced a great challenge, He met it with prayer and Scripture. He steeled Himself for the agony of the Passion with hours of prayer. I have not met any adversity that I could not face when I meet it with God's Word and presence in prayer. This is one place where it is okay to be constantly "plugged in."

GOD'S TAKE

Pray in the Spirit at all times and on every occasion. Stay alert and be persistent in your prayers for all believers everywhere.

EPHESIANS 6:18

A DOSE OF GRACE

The grace suggestion for this chapter is to be intentionally prayerful all day. When you think of a friend or family member, breathe a prayer for that person. When you watch or listen to the news, pray for those who are talked about (yes, even those you disagree with!). When you pass by a mom struggling with her child, pray for her. When someone is rude to you, pray for him. Pray for your day and your actions, your thoughts and your responses. They don't have to be articulately spoken words. Just align your thoughts into prayerful submission to God's character. I believe a not-so-surprising thing will happen. Your attitude will get better, and your circumstances, even when unchanged, will seem less bothersome.

CHAPTER 18

LET GOD LOVE YOU

We should be astonished at the goodness of God, stunned that he should bother to call us by name, our mouths wide open at his love, bewildered that at this very moment we are standing on holy ground.

BRENNAN MANNING[1]

GRANDKIDS ARE SUCH A GIFT. There is something special about the relationship between grandparents and grandchildren. During our home-team gatherings, we share our life stories, and more often than not someone expresses how a grandparent—usually a grandmother—made a significant impact on his or her faith journey. That was my experience with my dad's mother.

My older sister, Sherry, and I called her Granny, and she was our first messenger of grace, although I did not realize that until later in life. Granny was always welcoming and grateful for one minute or many hours of my time. I never once felt guilty or unloved in her presence.

Granny earned extra money by taking on sewing projects, money which she would use to buy gifts for us. Whenever I came to see her, she always had baked something special for me. My favorite was her dried apple cake. She would dry apples from our local orchard on wooden and wire drying racks laid on the heating vents in the floor. Her house would have that wonderful smell of apple and cinnamon when you walked in, and when I sat down at the kitchen table, she would bring me a piece of cake with a smile on her face. She wanted nothing in return. She just loved me and showed it. She modeled grace.

When I got my driver's license, my visits to Granny Davis's house became more and more unannounced. I would run there when I was sad or afraid. She was my refuge. In her presence, I experienced unconditional love, more than in any other place in my early life.

I have her Bible, and I found an inscription inside when I was writing this book. Somehow I had missed it before. Granny had written, "David Burchett was married July 17, 1976, to a wonderful girl, Joni Banks. My prayer [is] they will always be happy." She signed it as if she expected I would discover it someday. I am grateful her prayer was and is being answered.

Granny would faithfully pray for our young family. Joni and I often tell the story of how desperately poor we were when our first child, Matt, came along. There were many times when we scavenged for coins to scrape together money for milk. Whenever we were most in need, a letter would arrive postmarked "Chillicothe, Ohio." In her distinctive scribble, Granny Davis would write a note of encouragement to us, accompanied by money from her sewing projects. Whether it was five dollars or twenty, it always seemed to be just what we needed to get by for that moment.

That was no accident. This was a woman who was dialed

in to the Holy Spirit, and she demonstrated the Psalm 139 principle that God knows our needs and moves before we have any idea. It gave Joni and me a very early and unforgettable example of how God provides. Now whenever we face uncertainty, we know that He provides, in part because of a five-foot-two dynamo of faith who showed us what faith and grace look like in real life.

Grandparenting may be one of the most important jobs you will ever have. I believe the role I have in the lives of my grandkids is a sacred role. I love every part of being Papa to them, but I have to admit I love the cuddle times the most. A good use of my phone is to scroll through photos of those moments with the grandkids—snuggling with Ethan, Bennett, and Clara sitting on my lap at the end of an active day, and baby Madeline with her head on my shoulder, burrowing into my heart.

I think that is such a wonderful earthly illustration of how God the Father wishes we would approach Him and accept His love. We are His adopted children, and He wants us to snuggle into His love and forgiveness.

> You have not received a spirit that makes you fearful slaves. Instead, you received God's Spirit when he adopted you as his own children. Now we call him, "Abba, Father."
> ROMANS 8:15

Perhaps it was my early church teaching—that God expects performance before blessings can be expected—that causes me to struggle with the concept that God loves me. I believe He can love others. I accept without question that He loves the homeless person living on the street and the struggling inner-city mom trying to hold her family together. But I am less sure that He always loves me.

After all, I know me. I know what lies hidden in my heart. I know my reactions. I know my thoughts. God knows all of that too. So in the sad and difficult moments, I wonder how He could possibly love me. Those old voices remind me that when you get past my facade, there is not a lot to like.

Perhaps that is your struggle as well.

Recently I wrote about my extremely brief theater career in high school, when I played the lead in the musical *Man of La Mancha*. Little did I know that my role of Don Quixote was a glimpse into the future about how I would become a skinny, occasionally delusional old man with impossible dreams.

The play is based on Miguel de Cervantes's seventeenth-century novel *Don Quixote*. The musical unfolds as a play within a play, performed by Cervantes and his fellow prisoners, as he awaits a hearing with the Spanish Inquisition. Cervantes takes on the character of knight-errant Don Quixote.

How the tender, seemingly detached-from-reality character views the harlot Aldonza is the primary story line. Quixote sees a lady and gentle spirit buried deep beneath her hardened and bitter exterior. Eventually, she believes what the man from La Mancha says about her, and she leaves her old identity behind. Don Quixote serves as an agent of grace in her life.

One of the most powerful scenes in the play can also be applied to our Christian journey. Quixote's family and acquaintances plot how to quietly put him away because he has become an embarrassment to them. While saying how they are "only thinking of him," they plan to actually stop Don Quixote by confronting him in a room of mirrors.

When he sees who he really is—not a courageous knight, but merely a foolish old man—he will have to face the truth. They will indict him with their cynical view of reality.

> *Look, Don Quixote. Look in the mirror of reality*
> *and behold things as they truly are.*

They force Quixote to confront the reflection and admit that he is not a knight but rather a fraud pretending to be brave. The accuser in the play is called the Knight of Mirrors. He is a dark and foreboding character set on exposing Quixote and destroying his famous impossible dream.

Don't most of us have that fear of being exposed for who we perceive we really are to others? I have an accuser in my life named Satan who is more than willing to prey on that fear. Whenever I begin to trust and grow in grace, he holds up the mirror of accusation. If I rewrote the scene from *Man of La Mancha* as it has played out in my life, it would sound something like this:

> *Look, Dave Burchett. Look in the mirror of reality*
> *and behold things as they truly are.*
> *What do you see? A saint? A righteous man?*
> *Naught but a sinner. A man who desires to do the right*
> *   thing but does the opposite.*
> *How can you love this God and still fail so miserably?*
> *Look! You are a loser dressed for a masquerade called*
> *   church.*
> *See yourself as you truly are!*

For too many years I believed the accusations, without considering the question that Philip Yancey asks.

> Sociologists have a theory of the looking-glass self:
> you become what the most important person in your
> life (wife, father, boss, etc.) thinks you are. How
> would my life change if I truly believed the Bible's
> astounding words about God's love for me, if I
> looked in the mirror and saw what God sees?[2]

I am learning to look into the mirror and see someone that I accept by faith and not by my feelings. I see a saint. That's right. Many (maybe most) of Satan's accusations are true. But what I now see is a man who is a saint. I found forty references to *saints* in Paul's writings in the English Standard Version. From his additional descriptions, I am pretty sure that the recipients of his letters were not always behaving like saints. They were saints because of Christ, and not by meticulously following the law.

God sees those who trust Jesus as righteous, no matter how many accusations are thrown at them. Amazing.

> All praise to God, the Father of our Lord Jesus Christ,
> who has blessed us with every spiritual blessing in the
> heavenly realms because we are united with Christ. Even
> before he made the world, **God loved us and chose us
> in Christ to be holy and without fault in his eyes.** God
> decided in advance to adopt us into his own family by
> bringing us to himself through Jesus Christ.
>
> EPHESIANS 1:3-5 (EMPHASIS ADDED)

That is my (and your) identity as a follower of Jesus. Holy and without fault in His eyes. I will be accused again, probably sooner than later. But I am learning to simply say this to myself: "That is not who I am anymore. I am holy because of Christ."

When I forget that truth, I allow doubt, confusion, shame, and sadness to creep in. Not leaning on the finished work of Jesus as my strength and identity sets me up for a frustrating masquerade of faith.

There may be no element more important to living fully in the moment with God than accepting that I am loved by Him right now just as I am. That is so counterintuitive to how "love" so often works in my experience. I have talked with too many men who justify their extramarital relationships by saying they deserve more than their current marriage provides. It always hurts my heart because those they hurt deeply do not deserve to be wounded by betrayal. I try to never forget what I said on that July day more than forty years ago to my bride. I made vows to Joni Lynn Banks before God. I did not sign a contract with escape clauses based on my happiness at any given point in time.

The world speaks a different love language. "I will love you while you are attractive." "I will love you when you make me happy." "I will love you when you do what I ask you to do." Human love almost always includes conditional elements. That is not God's love.

> The LORD your God is in your midst;
>   he is a warrior who can deliver.
> He takes great delight in you;
>   he renews you by his love;
>   he shouts for joy over you.
>
> ZEPHANIAH 3:17, NET

The attributes of God's love are mind boggling. It is personal. You and I can relate to God the Creator of the universe as our Father. Think about that. I mean *really* think about that.

I am conditioned to believe that if something seems too good to be true, then I am being deceived. That is what Satan would have me believe. But the stunning radicality of grace is that what seems to be too good to be true is more true than I can imagine. This unconditional love from God is unrelated to the emotions, expectations, and desires that taint my human love. God's love is offered to the undeserving and unworthy, regardless of status, gender, color, nationality, wealth, or educational achievement.

God loves us first. He is the One who woos us to Him. He is the patient, loving Father who never leaves and is always there when His child finally comes home.

This love is ours to receive. We don't have to do a single thing except bring our wounds and sins to the loving Great Physician. When I believe that Christ died for the sins of the world, I am moved. When I believe that Christ died for my sins, I am changed.

I am choosing to believe that today.

GOD'S TAKE

Dear friends, let us continue to love one another, for love comes from God. Anyone who loves is a child of God and knows God. But anyone who does not love does not know God, for God is love. God showed how much he loved us by sending his one and only Son into the world so that we might have eternal life through him. This is real love—not that we loved God, but that he loved us and sent his Son as a sacrifice to take away our sins.

I JOHN 4:7-10

A DOSE OF GRACE

Allow God to love you today. You do not have to earn that love. You are adopted and worthy because of Jesus. Open your arms and your heart to His love. Feelings ebb and flow, but God's feelings for His children are an eternal fountain of grace. Jump in the fountain today and splash around. Laugh. Rejoice. You are a cherished and adored child of the King. Live like it.

CHAPTER 19

GETTING OUTSIDE
OF YOURSELF

God never said that the journey would be easy,
but He did say that the arrival would be worthwhile.

MAX LUCADO

FOR YEARS I WENT THROUGH emotional ups and downs that Joni described as my "funks." She walked on relational eggshells when I was going through these moods. Finally, I agreed to try medication. Within two weeks, my bride greeted me in the morning with a sentence I will never forget.

"I like you again."

She had never stopped loving me, but I had become difficult to like at times. That was many years ago. I am delighted to report that she still loves and still generally likes me. Hey, it's not a miracle drug!

If I may borrow a line from a Monty Python skit, I proclaim that "I'm getting better."[1] But I have learned a bit about accepting and playing the hand that has been dealt to me. In the movie *Shadowlands*, C. S. Lewis is portrayed as saying, "Experience is a brutal teacher. But you learn, my God you learn."[2] Yes, you do.

One of my challenges over the years has been obsessing about my circumstances. And I do mean obsessing. I had some really hard lessons to learn about my spiritual and emotionally unhealthy obsessions with people who wronged me. Being honest about seeing if medication could help was important and instructive. The medicine did a couple of things. It leveled out my moods and helped me to not obsess about problems or difficult people. I have since researched the ADD brain and found that my brain scan would look different from most people's. I can hear my blog readers' joint response: "Really? You are not normal? Who knew?"

Moodiness and depression are often caused by brain chemistry that goes askew. In my case, the chemical messenger seratonin was not properly regulated. The medication corrected that with pretty amazing results. Not only did Joni like me more (which was a rather huge benefit), but it also helped me discern which struggles were spiritual battles and which ones were simply brain chemistry issues. That was one of the most liberating experiences in my journey. For years, I felt so guilty that I couldn't shake these emotional blahs by trying harder to trust God with my mood. When my brain-chemistry playing field was leveled, I could recognize when the problem was truly in my heart.

My early pattern was predictable. Get sad. Try harder. Feel guilty. Listen to the old mental tapes telling me that I always do this and I always will. Get dog piled by Satan. Withdraw into hiddenness and sadness and grumpiness. Hard to imagine why my wife didn't like me much during those times.

Depression can be caused by many things. Medication

may not be the answer for everyone, and it is not the only tool in the healing tool kit. But it can be a tool that is helpful. I would ask those who are so critical of these medications to answer these questions: If your cholesterol is too high, does it show a lack of trust in God to take medication to lower those levels? Could God not lower your LDL level without the crutch of medication if you simply trusted him more? I absolutely believe that God could do that. But I would still do what is medically prudent while believing that God is ultimately in control of my health. My brain chemistry is stable enough now to know that just makes sense.

Every person who wonders if his or her struggles might be a brain chemistry issue should find a competent and trusted doctor to evaluate the particular situation. Ask those who love you and have your back what they think. One of my issues before medication was an inability to see myself accurately. I needed others I could trust to help with that.

Some people need medication and counseling. Some need counseling alone. We all need to be loved and nurtured through God's Word to walk through the valleys of life. Paul told us to "rejoice with those who rejoice; mourn with those who mourn" (Romans 12:15). We need to walk alongside those who are sad and lonely and depressed. And I know that is not easy.

Life's circumstances can be hard to accept for even the most mentally healthy—if such people actually exist. I wanted to take that brief detour to acknowledge that navigating this life is complex. When I encourage you to look outside yourself to serve others, I want to be sensitive to the fact that some need a little help to get over sadness and depression.

But the truth is that many of us are just dealing with everyday frustrations and challenges. It is so easy to get caught up in our own resentments that we lose sight of the sacred all around us. And it is very difficult to see challenging circumstances as critical building blocks to spiritual maturity.

Paul was dealt some pretty bad hands during his missionary journeys. I suspect it would have been easy for him to question God about his lot. After all, it was God who very aggressively recruited Paul onto the team while he was traveling to Damascus. But Paul knew that difficulties are a vital part of the spiritual-growth program. Here is what he wrote from prison:

> I rejoiced greatly in the Lord that at last you renewed your concern for me. Indeed, you were concerned, but you had no opportunity to show it. I am not saying this because I am in need, for I have learned to be content whatever the circumstances. I know what it is to be in need, and I know what it is to have plenty. I have learned the secret of being content in any and every situation, whether well fed or hungry, whether living in plenty or in want.
>
> PHILIPPIANS 4:10-12, NIV

I am so grateful that Paul did not write "I *am* content" and "I *know* the secret," even though those words could have been true. He was divinely inspired to honestly write that he had *learned* to be content and he had *learned* the secret. It did not come naturally or easily to Paul either.

Contentment is learning how to be present with Jesus in every circumstance. Our nature is to not enjoy the moment at hand when it is not ideal. We focus on whatever is bothering us. We long for comfort and fail to look for the blessings that usually surround us. Maybe what we really need is the lesson of the circumstance.

I wrote a bit about our rambunctious, i.e., crazy golden retriever Charlie in my last book. Perhaps one Charlie story I didn't tell there illustrates how we can find comfort in a worrisome moment.

Charlie developed a large benign tumor under his front leg that made walking difficult. We took him in for what would be a rather serious surgery at his ripe old canine age of twelve. The vet did a masterful job in removing the growth and taking care of Charlie. He spent the night at the clinic, and in the morning it was time to bring Charlie home. Joni and I were waiting in the reception area, and when Charlie shuffled out, I was taken aback by his appearance. Charlie was trembling, frightened, and apparently in some pain. His head was down and his tail that was always in perpetual motion was strangely stilled. He seemed confused and disoriented.

I walked over to Charlie and gently touched him. Immediately, he quit trembling and made a valiant attempt to wag his tail. We carefully got him into the car and took him home to heal.

Now, as I reflect on that scene, Charlie's reaction to my touch and mere presence was a wonderful illustration of how Jesus comforts (or desires to comfort) me. When I (his master) touched Charlie, he was comforted. His pain was not gone. He was still frightened. He was still a bit disoriented and unsure. Charlie's circumstances hadn't really changed at all. But he knew that his master was there, and that made it better.

What a picture that is of how the touch of Jesus enables us to respond when we are frightened about the future. We need to remind ourselves that Jesus never promised that all trouble would vanish when we believe in Him. In fact, the opposite often happens.

Jesus did promise that He would be there and that His presence would be enough. But I always want to avoid pain and difficult situations. Even as I desire changed situations, the quiet voice of God is seeking a changed *me*. Paul never asked for different circumstances for those he prayed for in his letters. He asked for patience, thanksgiving, joy, hope, confidence, and trust, because he knew that growing in those traits would be enough for those reading his words to endure whatever life threw at them.

This journey was never promised to be comfortable. But I have often tried to make it that. Comfy Christianity is easy in America. We encounter a store clerk who won't say "Merry Christmas," and we think we are being persecuted. God help us. We send checks instead of serving hands-on. But according to most data about charitable giving, we don't even do that very well.

God has called me (and you) to give and to serve. In the Civil War the wealthy paid poor men to "serve" for them on the battlefield. I remember having such disdain when I read that bit of history. But don't I do the same thing in my Christian journey? I feel really good if I pay a missionary to go reach the world with the message of Jesus. I feel like I am godly if I give to the church so the "professionals" can do ministry. If I give to a homeless shelter, I can assuage my guilt.

But God is asking me to do both. Give and serve. Maybe not to be an overseas missionary, but certainly to reach out to my neighbor and my community. I was not created to live in a safe bunker of climate-controlled Christianity. Jesus is not safe. Following Him will take you out of the comfort zone and into the messy world of ministry.

It can be a simple thing. Our pastor, Jeff Denton, has

served in a unique way every Christmas morning since he and his wife, Deanna, got married. Every year they take musical instruments and visit a senior citizens' facility to sing Christmas songs. When their children Amelia and J.J. came on the scene, they began to participate too, showing love to folks who might otherwise be completely alone on this day. We have had the chance to join the Dentons and others from our worship community a few times. I always feel a little awkward when I arrive, but I walk away feeling warmed by grateful faces that stick in my mind. Witnessing the look of appreciation and the smiles of recognition as these folks hear carols and traditional Christmas songs is heartwarming. Letting a few people know they are not forgotten and they are valued is a wonderful gift to give to Jesus on His birthday.

Valuing everyone is how Jesus lived. He modeled that with women, children, people with physical and mental challenges, lepers, social outcasts, and sinners. He served the weak and loved the unloved. He created the template for the New Testament church.

How did the early church explode and multiply against all odds? By serving selflessly, recklessly, and fearlessly. There was nothing comfortable about spreading the news about Jesus in the days, months, and years after His resurrection. The apostles understood after the Cross what Jesus had been trying to tell them earlier. That the world measures greatness on an entirely different scale from the one that God uses.

Remember that debate among the apostles? They had the criteria for greatness completely wrong.

They began to argue among themselves about who would be the greatest among them. Jesus told them, "In this world the kings and great men lord it over their people, yet they are called 'friends of the people.' But among you it will be different. **Those who are the greatest among you should take the lowest rank, and the leader should be like a servant.** Who is more important, the one who sits at the table or the one who serves? The one who sits at the table, of course. But not here! For I am among you as one who serves."

LUKE 22:24-27 (EMPHASIS ADDED)

The best way to take your eyes off your own circumstances is to serve others. Even as Jesus faced the horror of the Cross, He was serving others.

Martin Luther King Jr. said it well: "Everybody can be great . . . because anybody can serve. You don't have to have a college degree to serve. You don't have to make your subject and verb agree to serve. You only need a heart full of grace. A soul generated by love."[3]

Every person in the body of Christ can serve in some way. It may be running errands for a seasoned citizen who can no longer drive. It may be babysitting for a harried young mom. It may be providing a meal to a family dealing with illness. It may be calling or visiting a lonely person. Sometimes listening is one of the greatest ways to serve others. Maybe one subtle way to serve is simply appreciating those people whom you work and live with in community.

The Carrot Principle, a book by Adrian Gostick and Chester Elton, determined that appreciation might well be the missing accelerator for happiness and self-esteem. Based on a ten-year study in which two hundred thousand people were interviewed, the authors conclude that appreciation tops the list of things employees say they want from their bosses. For those who worked in offices with high morale, an amazing

94 percent reported that they were shown appreciation. Not surprisingly, when employees quit, nearly 80 percent cited lack of appreciation as the number one reason.[4]

We have a fundamental need to be affirmed. The authors of *The Carrot Principle* were surprised at how sparingly this blessing is given to others. I suspect it is often in short supply in our faith communities as well. That is a wonderful way you can serve others. Simply affirm and bless them in their gifts and skills.

One of my spiritual heroes is author John Lynch. He is funny, insightful, and smarter than he lets on. His insights on the topic of grace in books like *The Cure* have been used by God to change my spiritual journey profoundly. John is a master of affirmation, and he makes you feel like the most important person he has ever met. What a gift to take the time to make those God brings along your path feel valued and needed!

Serving can be the smallest gesture, or it can be a self-less response to a crisis. I absolutely love the slogan that the Salvation Army has been using recently: "We combat natural disasters with Acts of God."

That is a powerful thought. We as the body of Christ commit "acts of God" by loving, helping, and healing those who suffer from a disaster, or sometimes just from life. My insurance policy outlines "acts of God" as a way to diminish liability. My understanding of God's Word is that we have *increased* liability when others need help.

I pray that I will be willing to commit an "act of God" whenever I see a hurting person. When a student is struggling and needs mentoring, you can commit an "act of God." When a family does not have money for gifts at Christmas, your "act of God" will make the difference. When someone is feeling blue, you can affirm and lift that person's spirits by simply being present and caring. Jesus taught that these things we do are acts for God.

> The king will say to those on his right, "Come, you who are blessed by my Father, inherit the kingdom prepared for you from the foundation of the world. For I was hungry and you gave Me something to eat; I was thirsty and you gave Me something to drink; I was a stranger and you invited Me in; naked, and you clothed Me; I was sick, and you visited Me; I was in prison, and you came to Me."
>
> Then the righteous will answer Him, "Lord, when did we see You hungry, and feed you, or thirsty, and give You something to drink? And when did we see You a stranger, and invite you in, or naked, and clothe you? When did we see You sick, or in prison, and come to You?" The King will answer and say to them, "Truly I say to you, to the extent that you did it to one of these brothers of Mine, even the least of them, you did it to Me."
>
> MATTHEW 25:34-40, NASB

Part of the journey to disconnect from devices and reconnect to God and others is simple. Get outside yourself by serving and affirming others. The rewards are remarkable.

GOD'S TAKE

Don't forget to do good and to share with those in need. These are the sacrifices that please God.

HEBREWS 13:16

A DOSE OF GRACE

There are a thousand ways to serve others, and it is a healthy way to get outside yourself and reduce your obsession over life's circumstances. The smallest act of service means more than the grandest intention to serve, so look for ways to commit "acts of God" today. Often when you serve others, you end up feeling more blessed than the ones you have made the effort to bless. Give it a try.

CHAPTER 20

WORDS DO MATTER

Be careful with your words. Once they are said,
they can be only forgiven, not forgotten.

UNKNOWN

DADISM IS AN ACTUAL TERM for memorable things fathers say to their children. Whenever my boys get together, they tease me about my dad jokes that were (and are) an ongoing source of embarrassment for them. Here are some examples of my witty banter:

Waiter: "Here is your credit card receipt, Mr. Burchett."

Me: (looking surprised): "It went through?"

Boys: Groans from under table.

In the early 1950s, the Boy Scouts erected two hundred miniature Statues of Liberty around the country. The copper replicas stand about eight-and-a-half feet tall without the base. One of them was erected on Highway 80 near Forney, Texas, and we passed the mini–Miss Liberty every year on our way to cut down the family Christmas tree.

> Me: (excited): "Look, guys! It's the Statue of Liberty!" (Dad-joke pause) "I always thought it was bigger than that."

> Boys: Audible sounds of eyes rolling.

I especially exasperated them when I joked with their friends. At the time, they didn't understand that these pithy sayings and bad jokes are a part of the unwritten rules of fatherhood. When their children get to the point where they can groan at dad jokes, I fully expect them to carry on the tradition. When I spot that happening, I will be sure to send them this parenting tweet from comedian Jim Gaffigan:

> Me to my son: You remind me of me.

> Son: That's just mean.[1]

I am sure if you interviewed my three sons, a couple of my dadism philosophies would also be mentioned.

"Life isn't fair" would have to be in the top three. They learned to quit saying that something wasn't fair, because I readily agreed with them. I hope they would now agree that understanding that truth is important to dealing with the things life throws at you.

The other one I suspect they would readily recite is "Burchetts don't quit." I did not let them back out of commitments just because they didn't like the way things were going. I remember Scott being paired up on his first baseball team with a coach who did not understand how to relate to him at all. It was frustrating for Scott (and Joni and me), but we did not entertain the option of quitting. It was understood that you finished what you started.

That frustrating season for Scott led me into coaching him in baseball and basketball. Joni and I lived at baseball fields and school gyms over the years with Matt, Scott, and Brett. Thankfully, I have seen perseverance pay off in many ways in all my sons' lives.

I had a lot of fun with my boys when they were growing up. I said a lot of good things and even some funny things now and then. I regret some of the things I said to them in anger and frustration. Words are powerful, and I am only now really understanding the impact words can have on a heart.

I had to steel myself when I started writing and being vulnerable about my life and faith. To be honest, 95 percent of the comments, reviews, and responses I receive from readers are kind. But my nature tends to forget those and focus on the angry and mean comments. One person who read my book *Stay* surmised I was a really bad person because I had to leave town when my wonderful canine friend Hannah was near the end. The reader decided that I cared more about work than about my dog and said she couldn't finish the book because of my insensitivity. That is a lot of judgment from a person who doesn't know me at all. As much as I tried not to, I let it bother me.

When it comes to social media, people seem to be on the attack all the time. We say truly ugly things and assign terrible motives to people we don't know. I quit going negative on social media many years ago. I affirm where I can and stay silent when I cannot. I just don't understand what satisfaction people get from savaging someone or something from the safe bunker of the Internet. Maybe I should develop an app that prompts you to pray before you hit send.

The meaning of words can change over the years. Sometimes we diminish the power of words by overuse and misuse. One annoying example for me is the word *awesome*. If a breakfast sandwich is awesome, then what descriptor can you possibly pull out for a sunset that evening? Another word I would like to reclaim and limit is *hate*. *Hate* is a powerful and deeply affecting word. But we toss it around so casually that it makes me wince. We hate everything from Congress to broccoli. I am not sure this chapter would have made it into this book if my journey had been taken in a nonpolitical year.

I am saddened, sickened, disturbed, and frightened at how the word *hate* is being hurled around in our national discourse. Red-faced people running for office spew vitriol at those they disagree with. It can be an honest and complicated issue that candidates are reacting to, but they reduce the debate to hating their opponents.

Author James Baldwin made this insightful observation: "I imagine one of the reasons people cling to their hates so stubbornly is because they sense, once hate is gone, they will be forced to deal with pain."[2]

Isn't that the truth? It is so much easier to demonize than to understand. It is up to me and to you to change the discourse. We need to start by allowing God to be the one who defines hate. After all, He does have that righteous and holy thing on His résumé.

In the book of Proverbs, there is a list of seven things that God hates:

Eyes that are arrogant,
a tongue that lies,
hands that murder the innocent,
a heart that hatches evil plots,
feet that race down a wicked track,
a mouth that lies under oath,
a troublemaker in the family.
PROVERBS 6:17-19, MSG

It is heartbreaking that we, the body of Christ, have communicated a very different list of what we think God hates most. Perhaps we do that because the list above deals with the darkness in our own hearts. It is far easier to judge sin that isn't my issue than to do the painful work of confronting my own sin. Philip Yancey quotes a friend on his blog as saying, "Christians get very angry toward other Christians who sin differently than they do."[3]

And, inexplicably, we get incredibly angry at people who sin but who do not share our hope in Jesus. What in the world do we expect them to do? Isn't that part of why God graciously allows us another day, so that we can be light to those who do not share our faith?

Shouldn't step one for us as believers be to see how many items on this list of things that God hates still lurk in our own hearts? Let's review:

1. *Eyes that are arrogant.* Do I see myself as more important than others? Do I think I am "better" than others because I don't personally struggle with some particular sin? If I do that, then I am forgetting (again) that anything good in me is because of Christ. I don't think C. S. Lewis exaggerated the

impact of arrogance and pride: "Unchastity, anger, greed, drunkenness, and all that, are mere flea bites in comparison: it was through Pride that the devil became the devil: Pride leads to every other vice: it is the complete anti-God state of mind. . . . It is Pride which has been the chief cause of misery in every nation and every family since the world began."[4]

2. *A tongue that lies.* I relish the fact checkers who follow our politicians around and expose their subtle or not-so-subtle manipulations of the truth. Perhaps I should be more concerned about allowing the fact-checking truth of the Holy Spirit to examine my statements and thoughts about others.

3. *Hands that murder the innocent.* I tend to pat myself on the back and move to number four on this one. I have not murdered an innocent person directly. But Jesus upped the ante during the Sermon on the Mount with a "not so fast, my friends" interpretation. In Matthew 5:21-24, Jesus says that hating someone in your heart without being willing to offer forgiveness is sin. John says that "anyone who hates another brother or sister is really a murderer at heart" (1 John 3:15). I am sobered that my lack of involved concern for suffering people around the world contributes to innocents being harmed and murdered.

4. *A heart that hatches evil plots.* Anytime I try to manipulate a situation or person to harm him or her (or the cause), it is sin.

> The human heart is the most deceitful of all things,
>   and desperately wicked.
> Who really knows how bad it is?
> JEREMIAH 17:9

That verse is not written to be a depressing buzzkill that will make me hate myself. That honest assessment instructs me to carefully align my heart and mind to God's Word to help prevent bad thoughts and actions.

5. *Feet that race down a wicked track.* Followers of Jesus should have some restraint before we act or react. The old line about how "the main exercises for churchgoers are jumping to conclusions and running others down" can be sadly true. That should never be the modus operandi for Christians. Here is a good little reminder from the Owner's Manual:

> So I say, let the Holy Spirit guide your lives. Then you won't be doing what your sinful nature craves.
> GALATIANS 5:16

6. *A mouth that lies under oath.* My first response? How is this different from having a lying tongue? But the more I reflect on it, I believe this relates to testifying falsely and causing someone to be punished unjustly. Slanderous and hurtful gossip passed along via social media is a modern example of how we can perpetuate untruths. Bearing false witness made its way into the top-ten list that Moses was given by God.

7. *A troublemaker in the family.* I am not talking about a sibling stirring up trouble with his little brother or sister. God's desire is for brothers and sisters in His family to live in unity. I will have disagreements, but I am instructed to work them out and forgive. The person who says, "If you do not agree with my position on this topic, I will cause trouble, leave, or some lethal combination of those two actions" is the

object of this text. I pray that I am never that person. Jesus addressed the positive side of this:

> God blesses those who work for peace,
> for they will be called the children of God.
> MATTHEW 5:9

Does this list look anything like the list of things that we say God hates to many nonchurchgoers? To be sure, there are other sins that go against God's perfect plan and Word. But the consistent thing that I keep confronting is that He is annoyingly more concerned about my heart than about the actions of others. God is not attention deficit, and I cannot distract Him with a shiny sign condemning someone else's sin. The politician's favorite tactic of justifying bad behavior with other bad behavior does not work with a holy God. Frankly, I am grateful He loves me too much to give me a pass on my blindness.

Pastor Mark Mitchell is one of many people who has reflected on Rabbi Joseph Telushkin's assessment of the power of words.

> Rabbi Telushkin, author of *Words That Hurt, Words That Heal,* has lectured throughout this country on the powerful, often negative impact of words. He often asks audiences if they can go 24 hours without saying any unkind words about, or to, another person. Invariably, a small number of listeners raise their hands, signifying "Yes." Others laugh, and quite a few call out, "No!"
>
> Telushkin responds, "Those who can't answer 'yes' must recognize that you have a serious problem. If

you can't go 24 hours without drinking liquor, you're addicted to alcohol. If you can't go 24 hours without smoking, you're addicted to nicotine. So if you can't go 24 hours without saying unkind words about others, then you've lost control over your tongue."[5]

Perhaps I am more finely tuned because of this journey to connect more with God and others, but it seems that people talk a lot about things and people they detest. I realize that unplugging from the device is very helpful in this regard because a lot of hate is being disseminated via social media and the Internet in general. *Hate* is a very serious word to use when talking about anyone, and especially another believer. As Christians, we simply do not have that option.

> If someone says, "I love God," but hates a fellow believer, that person is a liar; for if we don't love people we can see, how can we love God, whom we cannot see?
>
> 1 JOHN 4:20

> If anyone claims, "I am living in the light," but hates a fellow believer, that person is still living in darkness.
>
> 1 JOHN 2:9

Ouch. It's very clear—and uncomfortable to hear—that I need to pray for those I disagree with in the faith community.

But beyond that, I think we need to be extraordinarily prayerful about throwing the hate card at anyone. I would suggest that we often allow ourselves to slip from hating the sin to hating the sinner as well. A wise man tells us that "the fear of the LORD is to hate evil. Pride and arrogance and the way of evil and the perverted mouth I hate" (Proverbs 8:13, NASB).

All of those—pride, arrogance, the way of evil, and perverted speech—are attitudes, not folks. We have a really hard time separating those two, and we need to be cautious about flinging around the "hate the sin and not the sinner" cliché. I need to work at that distinction in love.

We certainly see the first half of this proverb played out every day on cable news:

Hatred stirs up strife,
    but love covers all offenses.
PROVERBS 10:12, ESV

The second half of this proverb has been demonstrated by a few brave souls in my lifetime. Martin Luther King Jr. had some legitimate reasons to hate, but he chose not to. His words have not lost their power: "I have decided to stick with love. Hate is too great a burden to bear."[6]

Another courageous African American, Booker T. Washington, made a similar choice. "I will permit no man to narrow and degrade my soul by making me hate him."[7]

I know there are some people who are so evil that they seem unredeemable outside of a true miracle. But I have found that the majority of folks who disagree with me are generally decent people, when I take the time to hear their stories and get to know them. We hate people we don't know and, without a doubt, that suspicious attitude prevents us from ever engaging with them.

I have decided to severely curtail my use of the word *hate*. I am making the choice to permit no man to degrade my soul by making me hate. And for the spiritual hall monitors, be aware that I am not going squishy on sin. There are actions, attitudes, and sins that I hate.

I have to remind myself that the actions that make me angry are the result of our fallen nature and sin. Hating people will not fix either of those issues. I can't influence hearts by using inflammatory words. Words do matter. A lot.

GOD'S TAKE

**Love must be sincere.
Hate what is evil; cling to what is good.**

ROMANS 12:9, NIV

A DOSE OF GRACE

I am praying that we will choose not to use the word hate *in reference to people but rather only to describe sin and evil actions. I pray that we will choose not to hate people, and that we leave the judging of people to the One who is holy. Let's strive as a community of believers to use that word with great thought and discernment.*

CHAPTER 21

SOUNDS OF SILENCE

Let us be silent that we may hear the whisper of God.

RALPH WALDO EMERSON

I LOVE TO WATCH MAGGIE when she is overseeing her back-yard domain. Sometimes she goes to the fence and lets out a couple of deep-throated barks to let some perceived threat know that she is on duty. Or she patrols every inch of the yard, sniffing as if it is her first and not her one-thousandth time to do this. Sometimes she stops to growl at a feral cat behind the fence.

But the routine I love most is when she lies in the yard with head high, surveying her kingdom in silence. She is completely dialed in, listening for any disturbance that might need her attention. Maggie is most able to take in her world when she drops the barking and growling.

Well played, Maggie. You are doing something most of us humans have a difficult time mastering—simply being silent and observing God's world.

There is hardly ever a complete silence in our soul. God is whispering to us well-nigh incessantly. Whenever the sounds of the world die out in the soul, or sink low, then we hear these whisperings of God. He is always whispering to us, only we do not always hear, because of the noise, hurry, and distraction which life causes as it rushes on.[1]

Sounds like our lives, doesn't it? And yet that observation was written in the mid-1800s by hymn writer Frederick W. Faber. More than a century and a half later, it hasn't gotten quieter. It is hard to imagine that the sounds of the world are not exponentially more cacophonous today. Perhaps the bigger issue isn't that the world is noisier and more distracting than ever. The relational danger may be our ability to pull into the cocoon of noise-canceling headsets and remove ourselves completely from our surroundings. Sometimes it helps concentration to limit the noise. The challenge is to not let headphones and earbuds become another impediment to finding sacred moments.

Recently, I walked up to one of my younger television crew members and went through a very well-thought-out description of what we needed for the broadcast that night. I waited for his confirmation, but instead he turned, pulled out a well-hidden earbud, and looked surprised.

"What?"

I had no idea he was in another world while I was talking to him. He had no idea I was lurking right next to him and talking. It was no big deal. We laughed, and I repeated the instructions. Going forward, I did determine to first make eye contact with whomever I was talking to for the best results. It made me think about how often we miss moments of laughter or relational opportunities when we retreat from others.

Yesterday when I took Maggie for a walk, I instinctively reached for my phone and headset. Typically, I listen to music along the way. I can get lost in music, which is not a bad thing. But today I knew I needed something else. I needed to be quiet, reflective, and prayerful about some things that were troubling my soul.

To be honest, some tunes from my rock-and-roll days would have been a much-preferred course. But I knew I needed to think and pray. So while Maggie excitedly sniffed and explored, I prayed for a person who has been adversarial. Did I want to do that? Hardly. But I knew it was important, and I needed quiet to allow the Holy Spirit to speak to my heart. There is something healing and helpful in praying for those who oppose us. It reminds me that God is the One in control. When I trust that, I can relax.

My walk in silence was indeed soothing. It comes as no surprise to find that studies have shown that excessive noise releases stress hormones in the body. Daniel Gross writes, "People living in loud environments experience chronically elevated levels of stress hormones. . . . The word 'noise' comes from a Latin root meaning either queasiness or pain."[2]

It will also come as no surprise that the Owner's Manual addresses our need for silence and solitude.

Let all that I am wait quietly before God,
   for my hope is in him.
He alone is my rock and my salvation,
   my fortress where I will not be shaken.

PSALM 62:5-6

Perhaps the most consistent role model for the need for solitude and silence was Jesus.

> Very early in the morning, while it was still dark, Jesus got up, left the house and went off to a solitary place, where he prayed.
>
> MARK 1:35, NIV

> Jesus often withdrew to lonely places and prayed.
>
> LUKE 5:16, NIV

> Jesus went out to a mountainside to pray, and spent the night praying to God. When morning came, he called his disciples to him and chose twelve of them.
>
> LUKE 6:12-13, NIV

> Jesus, knowing that they intended to come and make him king by force, withdrew again to a mountain by himself.
>
> JOHN 6:15, NIV

Jesus understood the need to recenter and reconnect with the Father. He understood the power of quiet to be able to hear the voice of His Father. How can we think we are able to function spiritually and emotionally without occasional silence and solitude? Finding periods of quiet is different from seeking a day or extended time of Sabbath that we explored earlier. This is not something I am accomplished at.

I have probably had more intentional, undistracted time during this book project than I have had in years, if not ever. Noise becomes a habit. If I am alone, I need the television in the background or music in my ears. I am learning that sometimes I just need silence. Silence that used to make me feel a bit unsettled is now becoming a welcome respite to think and pray.

A. W. Tozer said that "only after all the noise has spent itself do we begin to hear in the silence of our heart, the still, small, mighty voice of God."[3]

That requires us to slow down, give up our perceived control, and simply be quiet. I can tell you it does not come naturally in this culture. And this is another reminder that devices can be a wonderful tool, but they must be silenced as well.

I don't know if it was my three-year-old granddaughter Clara's peeking at my manuscript that inspired her words of wisdom when she was having lunch with Joni and me recently. Before we sat down at the table, Clara had been playing with a toy cell phone. She dramatically turned off the sound and put the toy device facedown on the table.

"I calmed my phone!" Clara proclaimed.

Words for all of us to live by, sweetheart!

Being alone and quiet so you can hear the still voice of the Holy Spirit is about a heart attitude more than location. For me, there is one really important benefit of reflective quiet in the presence of God: it interrupts my typical prayer time of delivering a monologue to God. I was taught to make my requests known in prayer after a little perfunctory praise. I went down my list, and I was done. One-way conversation. I am outta here!

Forcing myself to be quiet gives me a chance to look inward. To see where I might need to allow the light of God's grace to shine on some dark area. I allow myself to be fully in the moment and not worried about tomorrow. I allow myself the time to reflect on who I am and how the Father looks at me. It clears my mind to clearly think about what needs to be done. I remind myself that I don't have to constantly manage and be in control.

Although we looked at Psalm 46:10 as a deterrent for busyness in chapter 3, I think it also applies to the idea of quieting down.

Be still, and know that I am God!

The Hebrew word for "be still" might be better translated as "cause yourselves to let go" or "let yourselves become weak."

Sitting quietly with my Bible open to a psalm invites the quiet voice to speak. Often there is nothing but stillness. Isn't that how a good relationship works? When you feel relaxed and protected with your spouse, you can have periods of silence that actually speak volumes about how you feel about each other. It is in quiet solitude with God that I am wholly present and available to Him. Is there a better indicator of affection than undivided attention?

If my mind is left unattended, it is like Maggie as a puppy. It runs randomly and without restraint. I have had to learn to slow down, unplug, and be still. And I have had a major surprise: I am really enjoying it.

I have practiced this discipline often on this journey. My prior history when writing is to research, research, research. To be sure, I have done a fair measure of background study while writing this book. But more often than usual, I have unplugged the device and turned off all the distracting noise-makers. I have sat in silence and meditated on what God is teaching me. I have thought about what I would like to communicate and asked the Holy Spirit to give me creative direction. Without fail, I have found an idea or a story in those moments of silence. It has been one of my biggest takeaways from this experiment.

It is a lesson I intend to build on. God is powerful enough to teach an old dog new tricks. I invite you to find a place to be quiet today. In the sounds of silence, God may very well meet you.

GOD'S TAKE

For God alone, O my soul, wait in silence, for my hope is from him.

PSALM 62:5, ESV

A DOSE OF GRACE

Find some time to give God your undivided and silent presence. Start with five or ten minutes. It may feel awkward. Simply tell God that you desire to be in His presence. Tell Him that you want to be attuned to His direction or correction. But most of all, tell God that you simply want to receive His love. Remember there is no condemnation if your mind wanders. This will take some practice, but it is worth it.

Afterword

THE BEST PRESENT
YOU CAN GIVE

The best things in life aren't things.

ART BUCHWALD

THERE IS A COUNTRY SONG by George Strait that laments how long it took him to figure out things in his life. The lyrics humorously admit that he was wrong about a lot of things and slow to the dance on many others. One of my favorite lyrics in that song is when he hears "What a Wonderful World" by Louis Armstrong and it brings a tear to his eye. "After all these years," Strait sings, he finally gets that song.

Me too. That song by Louis Armstrong sees the beauty in this sometimes ugly world. flowers, the blue sky, rainbows, smiles, handshakes, love, and babies crying. And like a modern psalmist, Armstrong sits back and with a smile in his distinctive voice proclaims to himself and others that it is a wonderful world. Martin Luther said that "God writes the gospel not in the Bible alone, but on trees, and flowers, and clouds, and stars." I believe that now more than ever.

We began this journey hoping that together we could find ways to eliminate distractions and examine attitudes that keep us from enjoying more connection to God and one another. Devices, busyness, worry, cynicism, and ingratitude were just a sampling of the external and internal things that keep us from enjoying the moment.

It has been an eye-opening, convicting, and humbling journey for your ill-equipped tour guide. But this has been an amazing personal experiment, and the process has changed me. I see people hypnotized by their phones, and I feel regret for what they are missing. Am I a hypocrite because I was that guy just a few months ago, or am I blessed to be finally waking up?

Now I am determined to not let the devil or devices (sometimes they are one and the same) rob me of a precious moment. I hear people complaining about insignificant things, and I want to take their hand and show them the blessings all around them. I hear pundits and others spewing hateful rhetoric, and I want to tell them to relax—God is in control. I read passionate and too often ugly responses on social media, and my heart hurts. We don't consider that we are attacking, demeaning, and demonizing a human created in the image of God. I look for any chance to show kindness, and I thank God that my circumstances are not bigger than He is.

Recently, I had a travel nightmare. My flight was delayed, and the updates were not particularly helpful. It had already been a long day, and the late arrival was unfortunate. But we finally took off, and I breathed a sigh of relief. I took a taxi to the hotel and trudged to the clerk at the desk. Somehow, there was no reservation logged for me. The hotel was completely full, and there were no rooms at the half-dozen or so hotels that the employee called.

My previous reaction would have been indignation. I might have reminded her about my "gold" status with that hotel chain. Without question I would have made the hotel clerk feel bad about how much I was being inconvenienced. I was never one to go off in anger, but I was entirely capable of cynical comments. But the lessons of this journey were fresh in my mind. *Be kind.* This is not her fault. *Be grateful.* This is not even a blip on the world-suffering scale. *Be confident.* God is in control, and this will work out.

I finally located a hotel not too far away and went about the fun task of finding a taxi in a small city at two o'clock in the morning. I finally checked in and smiled at how God gives pop quizzes when we are asking the Spirit to teach us. I had navigated that travel ordeal without raising my blood pressure or incriminating someone without knowing who messed up. I learned the next day that I was the guilty party who had forgotten to follow up to confirm the reservation. Thank You, God, that I did not blame a person who was merely doing her job and had done nothing wrong. Sadly, I have done that before. Perhaps I am learning that a truly happy person enjoys the scenery on life's detours.

Every day I am gifted with 86,400 seconds of precious time. I cannot possibly use all of it wisely. But I can invest more of that daily gift into my relationships with God and others. I can't draw interest on unused time to be used later. Time is far more valuable than the money we so doggedly pursue. I can lose all my money and make more later. But if I lose my time, it is gone forever.

Solomon actually beat me to this message by about three

thousand years, give or take. He decided that, all things considered, the best way to live is to enjoy the moment.

> After looking at the way things are on this earth, here's
> what I've decided is the best way to live: Take care
> of yourself, have a good time, and make the most of
> whatever job you have for as long as God gives you
> life. And that's about it. That's the human lot. Yes, we
> should make the most of what God gives, both the
> bounty and the capacity to enjoy it, accepting what's
> given and delighting in the work. It's God's gift! God
> deals out joy in the present, the *now*. It's useless to
> brood over how long we might live.
> ECCLESIASTES 5:18-20, MSG

Just this week I sent a consoling message to a friend. Her apparently healthy and robust father died without a moment of warning. Not to be maudlin, but that is the reality of this earthly existence. We don't know if we have tomorrow or even the rest of today.

Certainly we must be wise to plan and prepare for a long future. But we must also invest in now, in case that is what we are given. I was joking with some friends recently that I wished life were like a soccer match. At the end of my life, a referee would announce how much "extra" time I had before I actually died. One ornery friend looked at me and deadpanned, "What if you are currently on your extra time?" I may well be, and that gives me all the more motivation to live fully in the moment.

Maybe the message that resonates the most for me is that we cannot receive postdated grace. We cannot order grace for the future. We receive grace in the now. Grace is

God's greatest gift of my being present with Him. When we are disconnected or distracted, we miss that blessing of real-time grace.

If I had to write a one-sentence summary of what I learned on this odyssey, it would be very simple. *Spend focused time with those you love and with your God.* Speaker-writer Zig Ziglar wrote about spending time with loved ones. "One of these days you will say either, 'I wish I had,' or 'I'm glad I did.'"[1]

How heartbreaking would it be to find yourself at the end of this pilgrimage with the regret of "I wish I had" roiling in your soul? My heart's desire is that I will gratefully say, "I'm glad I did."

If you want to give the very best present to your spouse, kids, friends, and God, the grace challenge is simple. *Be present.* When you are with your spouse, put the phone away. While you are with the kids or grandkids, forget whatever is pressing at work. I have never forgotten what entrepreneur Mary Crowley said to me when we were discussing the challenge of parenting. Mary said she had one regret. "I wish I had answered at the first tug." That is simply being present.

If a friend is suffering, you can show no greater love than to simply be there for him or her. Not offering great theological insight or stories of your own or others' suffering. Just to be present.

When you talk to a friend, be present. Not looking around as if your friend is merely a temporary diversion before someone more compelling comes along. Darting eyes deny that you are present. Phone snubbing (phubbing) denies that the person you are with is truly your primary concern.

I wrote about the power of simple presence in my book *Stay*. We were going through an incredibly scary season after my wife was diagnosed with breast cancer. Here is an excerpt describing how our dog Hannah's presence comforted me.

During Joni's cancer, Hannah obviously had no idea why we were sad. She had no more understanding of Joni's disease than she would later have of her own prognosis. But she could sense our sorrow and she was present in the moment.

Joni's breast cancer treatment included surgery and a year of chemotherapy followed by weeks of radiation. We joked about our weekly dates at the "Slow-Drip Spa," but there was not much humor to be found in the aftermath of those sessions. Joni fought nausea and her plummeting white blood cell counts were dangerously low, compromising her recovery. One day after we returned home from Joni's chemotherapy session, she went straight to the bedroom, exhausted, to try to sleep off the nausea. I sat on the couch in our living room staring at nothing as I tried to process all that Joni was going through.

Hannah sensed my sadness but wasn't sure what to do. She walked by, looked at me, picked up a tennis ball, and brought it to me. I could see a hint of uncertainty in her eyes. I imagined a thought bubble appearing over her head with the message, "Would this help make you less sad?"

I tossed the ball to her but she did not play with the normal zeal that she had during our games of catch.

This day Hannah caught the ball, calmly brought it back, and gently dropped it in my lap. It was as if she was doing this for me and not her. She was giving me a few moments of respite from my fears. I don't recall another time that she played in that way.[2]

Hannah didn't know what to do, so she instinctively did the best possible thing. She was fully present. That is the best thing we can give to others. Nothing makes a person feel more valued than being fully present.

Being present is the best worship we can give to God. We can sing and raise hands in worship to God, and that is good. We can talk about His love and forgiveness, and that is good. But nothing communicates our adoration for God more than being fully present with Him.

The enemy will remind you over and over of all that needs to be done. He will remind you of past wounds and failures. It would be wise to remember a couple of things at this point. Jesus has experienced exactly what you are going through right now. He was tempted in the desert by Satan. He was tired, hungry, and lonely. Jesus experienced this trio of circumstances that often cause me to yield to temptation, and He conquered them with a simple strategy. Jesus focused on the Father and rebuked Satan with Scripture. First Jesus was tempted to gratify His extreme hunger by turning the stones into bread. Then the Accuser taunted Jesus to prove His divine status by throwing Himself off the Temple and being rescued by attending angels. *The Message* colorfully describes the third temptation of Jesus:

> For the third test, the Devil took him to the peak of a huge mountain. He gestured expansively, pointing out all the earth's kingdoms, how glorious they all were. Then he said, "They're yours—lock, stock, and barrel.

Just go down on your knees and worship me, and they're yours."

Jesus' refusal was curt: "Beat it, Satan!"

I cannot tell you how much I love the image of Jesus turning to the enemy and telling him to "beat it." That is a strategy I will replicate when I am facing temptation.

Dave's refusal was curt: "Beat it, Satan!"

The story continues:

He backed his rebuke with a third quotation from Deuteronomy: "Worship the Lord your God, and only him. Serve him with absolute single-heartedness."

The Test was over. The Devil left. And in his place, angels! Angels came and took care of Jesus' needs.

MATTHEW 4:8-11, MSG

There is so much good stuff in those verses. Jesus' rebuke was backed by the Word of God. That gave authority to the command to "beat it." I can have a colleague tell me that I should complete a task at work. I may or may not do it. I can have a peer tell me. I may or may not respond. But when the boss tells me to do it, the job will certainly get done. He or she has authority. I am under that authority to obey, unless I make the bad choice of not responding, which may mean I will be looking for another job. That is what was going on here. Satan has power, but it is limited. God has the authority, and Jesus simply used that power.

Serve Him with absolute single-heartedness.

Be present.

We cannot multitask and be fully present with God. Only

God is omnipresent. I have to work at it with focus, stillness, and attentiveness.

A few years ago I wrote a series of articles about leaving a legacy as a dad. I learned that what your children take away as favorite memories may be surprising. One of the questions I asked my sons was their favorite memories of time with me. I expected that they would remember the big trips we took together or some expensive outing. I was humbled by their responses:

> Firstborn son, Matt: "My favorite memories are throwing the baseball/football in the front yard of our Pecan Valley house, going to baseball games, and growing up around sports."
>
> Second-born son, Scott: "Playing catch in the backyard for hours on end, even when your knees hurt. Going to cut down Christmas trees every November and stopping at the Dairy Queen on the way home."
>
> Youngest son, Brett: "You coaching my sports teams and going to cut down the Christmas tree."

It was my being present that mattered. The memories that really mattered to them were things that cost me only time. Each of the boys felt valued when he felt I had sacrificed or made a special effort to be fully present. I thought the big things mattered the most, but I was wrong.

Another question I asked the boys was what they wish I had done differently. Their responses were consistent and convicting. I share this in the hope that young dads will take this to heart.

Matt: "I wish you could have been home more."

Scott: "I wish you could have been home more."

Brett: "I wish you could have been home more."

That still makes my heart hurt. That is what I wish I had done differently. I wish I would have been home more. I cannot change the past. God is gracious and loving. My relationships with all of my boys are wonderful, despite my misplaced priorities at times. Love does cover a multitude of sins. My sons know they are loved. They know they have my approval and respect. But now I know that they simply longed for me to be more consistently present.

Some anonymous person summed it up perfectly:

People who have a lot of money and no time we call "rich." People who have time but no money we call "poor." Yet the most precious gifts—love, friendship, time with loved ones—grow only in the sweet soil of unproductive time.

The world might call quiet moments of presence with God and others unproductive time. I am learning that there is no more productive way we can spend our time. Everything that truly matters springs from that presence-enriched soil.

My heavenly Father is always present. I just need to show up for Him. That is the essence of spiritual growth for me. Just showing up in humility every day, seeking His presence. I will stumble in this journey to be present. I probably will need a refresher course often. But I am confident beyond confident of one truth that Paul wrote to the church at Philippi, which is true for you and me today:

> I am certain that God, who began the good work within you, will continue his work until it is finally finished on the day when Christ Jesus returns.
>
> PHILIPPIANS 1:6

I am *waking up slowly* in this life. But one day, fairly soon, I will *wake up glorified*. I believe the epitaph written on Ruth Graham's tombstone will also describe my journey: "End of construction—thank you for your patience."

Acknowledgments

I WOULD LIKE TO THANK MY AGENT AND FRIEND, Don Jacobson, for his unusual involvement with this project. Generally, he takes my half-baked ideas and helps me refine them into something that is worth pitching to a publisher. He certainly did that with this book, but he went the extra mile for this volume.

For years Don talked about a book he wanted to personally write outlining how he was finally figuring out some things later in life. He wanted to call the book *Waking Up Slowly*. Sound familiar? When I sent this book proposal to Don, he called me and said, "I want you to use my title."

"I can't do that," I replied. "You have been holding on to that title for yourself for years." Don insisted that my book was worthy of his vision. So I humbly and gratefully accepted his gift. Thank you, Don, for your encouragement, patience, enthusiasm, and gentle prodding. Thank you for gifting me with your book title. It makes this release even more special.

I also would like to thank my television family. For three

decades I have worked with mostly freelance technicians, camera operators, and production folks. I have been blessed to be a part of a community that loves and takes care of one another in a way that could instruct many churches. I have seen thousands of dollars given to a coworker who was injured or sick, from folks who are often struggling to meet their own needs. That is special, and I am blessed to be a part of such a family. I think I understand why Jesus preferred to hang out with the regular folks and not the powerful and the rich. There is something authentic and special about these men and women. Thanks for the laughs, the love, the hard work, and the friendships over the years.

Special thanks to my church family at Waterbrook Bible Fellowship. Pastor Jeff Denton has been a wonderful friend, encourager, and public relations agent for my previous books. Pastor Steven Bramer, Don Moore, and the entire leadership team have made Waterbrook a welcoming place of grace that I am grateful to call home.

I would like to thank my home team community group for their constant prayer and encouragement through this difficult process of finishing a book during my busiest season. I know they have my back in prayer, and that is an amazing comfort. Thank you, Duke, Laura, Frank, Tricia, Norma, Fran, Darrell, Christine, Judy, Greg, Toni, Pam, Jim, and Aundi. You all are the best!

Thanks to our supper club of "experienced" friends who have loved Joni and me so well for many years. Thanks John, Vicki, Bob, Judy, Rich, Sharon, Billie, Karen, Nelson, and Suzie! I look forward to our next gathering.

Thanks to my dear friend Ed Underwood, who talks me off of the emotional ledge when I get discouraged and convinces me I have something to say.

Thanks to Kevin Butcher, who inspires me with his passion and deep love for God's people. Your heart has changed mine.

Thanks to John Frost, who is one of the most caring and encouraging men I have met on this journey. Your humor and insight have been a real gift for many years.

I am incredibly grateful to partner again with the folks at Tyndale House Publishers. Thanks to Jon Farrar in acquisitions for continuing to believe in me as a writer. Thanks to my editor Bonne Steffen who inexplicably took on a second project with me! Bonne, you are such a blessing with your ability to connect with my heart. Your patience, humor, honesty, and love have made this project vastly better than the first draft was. Thank you.

Special thanks to the three grace musketeers at TrueFaced. It was a God-designed encounter with John Lynch, Bruce McNicol, and Bill Thrall in San Diego many years ago that introduced me to the principles of grace and identity that rocked my faith world and reworked my walk with Jesus. Thank you. Thank you. Thank you.

Thanks to my wonderful sister, Sherry, who started our family faith journey when she became a follower of Jesus. Your remarkable strength through heartache and trials has been an inspiration to me. Love you, sis!

And a special thank you to my remarkable sons and their families.

Matt, thank you for always challenging me and our family to be more connected, authentic, and loving. Thanks for your humor, compassion, leadership, and kindness to everyone around you. You are a wonderful husband to Holly and dad to Ethan and Madeline.

Holly, thank you for loving my son and us so well. Your

joy, faith, talent, and kindness have been such a blessing to Joni and me.

Ethan, what a joy you are for Nana and Papa. Your enthusiasm, energy, and sheer joy of living keeps us young. We love you so much!

Madeline, we are just getting to know you, but it is clear that God has put a sweet, sweet spirit in your heart. Your smile melts me and I look forward to getting to know your heart more and more.

Scott, your courage, integrity, and wisdom are remarkable. Your dry and always-on-point barbs keep all of us grounded. Thanks for your commitment to your family and friends. You are a fantastic husband to Caroline and dad to Bennett and Clara.

Caroline, thank you for being such a great wife to my son and a mom to Bennett and Clara. I love your exuberant pursuit of your family, career, and faith. We love having you in the family.

Bennett and Clara, you two have brought so much laughter and love to our family. Bennett, I love your intensity, mischievous smile, and sweet cuddles. Clara, thanks for making even mundane moments an event with your smile and unique flair.

Brett, thank you for your heart for others. Your humor, passion, and zest for life are a joy to behold. We look forward to seeing what lies ahead for you, and wherever God leads you, I know you will be caring, compassionate, and successful. That is simply who you are.

I am blessed beyond measure by all of you.

Notes

INTRODUCTION

1. *It's a Wonderful Life* was released in 1947, directed by Frank Capra. The movie was inspired by "The Greatest Gift," a story by Philip Van Doren Stern.

CHAPTER 1: THE CURSE OF CULTURE

1. Alonzo Mancha, "Why You're Still Bored," *Daily Infographic*, November 7, 2014, http://www.dailyinfographic.com/why-youre-still-bored-infographic.

2. Ariana Eunjung Cha, "Scientists: How 'Phubbing' (or Phone Snubbing) Can Kill Your Romantic Relationship," *Washington Post*, October 5, 2015, http://www.washingtonpost.com/news/to-your-health/wp/2015/10/05/scientists-how-phubbing-or-phone-snubbing-can-kill-your-romantic-relationship.

3. See "take for granted," *Dictionary.com*, http://www.dictionary.com/browse/take--for--granted.

4. Ibid.

CHAPTER 2: HOW TO REVERSE STINKIN' THINKIN'

1. *Cambridge Advanced Learner's Dictionary*, http://dictionary.cambridge.org/us/dictionary/english/stinking-thinking.

2. Adapted from David D. Burns, *The Feeling Good Handbook* (New York: Plume, 1999), 8–11.

CHAPTER 3: BUSYNESS IS NOT NEXT TO GODLINESS

1. Tim Kreider, "The 'Busy' Trap," *New York Times*, June 30, 2012, http://opinionator.blogs.nytimes.com/2012/06/30/the-busy-trap.

2. Ibid.

3. Audrey Barrick, "Survey: Christians Worldwide Too Busy for God,"

Christian Post, July 30, 2007, http://www.christianpost.com4/news/survey
-christians-worldwide-too-busy-for-god-28677.

4. Ibid.

CHAPTER 4: THE ALL-IMPORTANT OWNER'S MANUAL

1. Dave Burchett, *Stay* (Carol Stream, IL: Tyndale, 2015), 181–82.
2. Tim Keller, in the sermon "Literalism: Isn't the Bible Historically Unreliable and Regressive?," *PreachingToday.com*, accessed October 25, 2016, http://preachingtoday.com/sermons/sermons/2010/may/literalism.html.
3. Ibid.
4. Carl Sagan, *The Dragons of Eden: Speculations on the Evolution of Human Intelligence* (New York: Ballantine Books, 1977), 23–25.
5. Ibid.
6. Francis Collins, "Collins: Why This Scientist Believes in God," *CNN.com*, April 6, 2007, http://cnn.com/2007/US/04/03/collins.commentary /index.html.

CHAPTER 5: OPENING THE GIFT OF GRACE

1. Nancy Spiegelberg, "If Only I Had Known You," in *Fanfare: A Celebration of Belief*, by Nancy Spiegelberg and Dorothy Purdy (Portland, OR: Multnomah Press, 1981).
2. Paul Donnan, combined tweets, May 21, 2016, https://twitter.com /pauldonnan.

CHAPTER 6: NEW EYE FOR AN OLD GUY

1. Betty Smith, *A Tree Grows in Brooklyn* (Philadelphia: Blackiston, 1943), 364.
2. O. M. Bakke, *When Children Became People: The Birth of Childhood in Early Christianity* (Minneapolis: Augsburg Fortress, 2005), 29.
3. Ibid., 31.
4. A. R. Colón with P. A. Colón, *A History of Children: A Socio-cultural Survey across Millennia* (Westport, CT: Greenwood Press, 2001), 104–106.

CHAPTER 7: TIME TO RETHINK SABBATH

1. Andy Crouch, *Playing God: Redeeming the Gift of Power* (Downers Grove, IL: InterVarsity Press, 2013), 254.
2. Judith Shulevitz, "Bring Back the Sabbath," *New York Times*, March 2, 2003.
3. Wendell Berry, foreword to Norman Wirzba, *Living the Sabbath* (Grand Rapids, MI: Brazos Press, 2006), 12.
4. Dallas Willard, *The Great Omission: Reclaiming Jesus's Essential Teachings on Discipleship* (New York: HarperCollins, 2006), 36.

CHAPTER 8: DON'T LET YOUR PAST STEAL YOUR PRESENT

1. E. L. Doctorow, "The Art of Fiction No. 94," *The Paris Review*, no. 101 (Winter 1986).
2. John Claypool, "The Future and Forgetting," Preaching Today, tape no. 109.
3. Warren W. Wiersbe, *Be Joyful: Even When Things Go Wrong, You Can Have Joy* (Colorado Springs: David C. Cook, 2008), 114, emphasis added.

CHAPTER 9: BEGRUDGINGLY

1. Melissa Dahl, "17 Things We Know About Forgiveness," *Science of Us*, March 10, 2015, http://nymag.com/scienceofus/2015/03/17-things-we-know-about-forgiveness.html.
2. Melissa Dahl, "Holding a Grudge May Literally Weigh You Down," *Science of Us*, January 9, 2015, http://nymag.com/scienceofus/2015/01/holding-a-grudge-may-literally-weigh-you-down.html.
3. Ibid. See also http://spp.sagepub.com/content/early/2014/12/23/1948550614564222.abstract.
4. Will Davis Jr., *10 Things Jesus Never Said: And Why You Should Stop Believing Them* (Grand Rapids, MI: Revell, 2011), 124.

CHAPTER 10: GRATITUDE RHYMES WITH ATTITUDE

1. Minda Zetlin, "Listening to Complainers Is Bad for Your Brain," *Inc.*, August 20, 2012, http://inc.com/minda-zetlin/listening-to-complainers-is-bad-for-your-brain.html.
2. Peter Robinson, *How Ronald Reagan Changed My Life* (New York: HarperCollins, 2004), 15–16.

CHAPTER 11: WORRYING STEALS THE MOMENT

1. Robert Leahy, *The Worry Cure* (New York: Random House, 2005), 109.
2. David Jeremiah, *Slaying the Giants in Your Life* (Nashville: Thomas Nelson, 2001), 67.
3. Helen Lemmel, "Turn Your Eyes upon Jesus," 1918.

CHAPTER 12: KINDNESS REALLY IS CONTAGIOUS

1. Roy B. Zuck, *The Speaker's Quote Book: Over 5,000 Illustrations and Quotations for All Occasions, Revised and Updated*, (Grand Rapids, MI: Kregel Publications, 2009), 289.
2. Casting Crowns, "If We Are the Body," *Casting Crowns* (Beach Street Records, 2003).
3. Marshall Goldsmith, "Goal 1, Mission 0," *Fast Company*, August 1, 2004, http://www.fastcompany.com/50082/goal-1-mission-0.
4. Emily Esfahani Smith, "Masters of Love," *The Atlantic*, June 12, 2014, http://www.theatlantic.com/health/archive/2014/06/happily-ever-after/372573/, emphasis added.

CHAPTER 13: DARE *NOT* TO COMPARE

1. Comedy Central, http://www.cc.com/jokes/4cr4bb/stand-up-mike-birbiglia--mike-birbiglia--dance-club-cure.
2. Ann Voskamp, "How the Hidden Dangers of Comparison Are Killing Us . . . (and Our Daughters): The Measuring Stick Principle," *Huffington Post*, November 8, 2013, http://www.huffingtonpost.com/ann-voskamp/how-the-hidden-dangers-of_b_4232320.html, emphasis added.
3. Anne Lamott's Facebook page, April 8, 2015, https://www.facebook.com/AnneLamott/posts/662177577245222.

CHAPTER 14: IF YOU'RE HAPPY AND YOU KNOW IT . . .

1. WorldCat.org, accessed November 2016.

2. John Calvin, *The Institutes of the Christian Religion*, rev. ed. (Peabody, MA: Hendrickson, 2007), 553.

3. "The Effect of Humor on Short-Term Memory in Older Adults: A New Component for Whole-Person Wellness," *Advances in Mind-Body Medicine* (Spring 2014):16–24.

4. "Stress Relief from Laughter? It's No Joke," *Mayo Clinic*, April 21, 2016, http://www.mayoclinic.org/healthy-lifestyle/stress-management /in-depth/stress-relief/art-20044456.

5. Susan Brink, "Is Laughter the Best Medicine?" *National Geographic*, June 7, 2014, http://news.nationalgeographic.com/news/2014/06/140606-laughter -jokes-medicine-health-science-laughing-yoga.

6. Ron Gutman, "The Untapped Power of Smiling," *Forbes*, March 22, 2011, http://www.forbes.com/sites/ericsavitz/2011/03/22/the-untapped-power -of-smiling/#6aff904c20d8.

7. Clinton Colmenares, "No Joke: Study Finds Laughing Can Burn Calories," *Reporter*, June 10, 2005, http://www.mc.vanderbilt.edu:8080/reporter/index .html?ID=4030.

CHAPTER 15: WE NEED A VILLAGE

1. Max Lucado, *Fearless: Imagine Your Life without Fear* (Nashville: Thomas Nelson, 2012), 144.

2. "Company Information," *Starbucks.com*, http://www.starbucks.com/about-us /company-information.

3. Philip Yancey, *What's So Amazing about Grace?* (Grand Rapids, MI: Zondervan, 1997), 274.

4. Interestingly enough, this year a new statue will be unveiled for the hundredth anniversary of Boys Town, featuring an African-American boy carrying a young girl on his back—with the same inscription. The statue of the two boys will be moved inside, added to the historical display. (Nancy Gaarder, "New Statue to Grace Boys Town Campus for 100th Anniversary," *Omaha World-Herald*, May 5, 2016, http://www.omaha.com/news/metro /new-statue-to-grace-boys-town-campus-for-th-anniversary/article _536e1202-1235-11e6-901f-6382686951dc.html.)

CHAPTER 16: THE DOUBT BOUT

1. Philip Yancey, "Faith and Doubt," PhilipYancey.com, http://philipyancey .com/q-and-a-topics/faith-and-doubt.

2. Timothy Keller, *The Reason for God: Belief in an Age of Skepticism* (New York: Penguin Books, 2008), xvi.

3. Steven Skiena and Charles B. Ward, "Who's Biggest? The 100 Most Significant Figures in History," *Time*, December 10, 2013, http://ideas .time.com/2013/12/10/whos-biggest-the-100-most-significant-figures -in-history.

4. Rich Mullins, "You Did Not Have a Home," *The Jesus Record* (Myrrh Records, 1998).

5. Adapted from Tom Barnette's post to Tony Evans's Facebook page, October 20, 2011, http://www.facebook.com/pastortonyevans/posts /297599133586527.

6. C. S. Lewis, *Mere Christianity* (New York: Macmillan, 1952), 55–56.

7. Timothy Keller, *The Reason for God* (New York: Penguin, 2008), 181.

CHAPTER 17: POWERED BY PRAYER

1. "Biscuits," *The Good Stuff*, March 30, 2016, http://www.thegoodstuffradioshow .com/#!Biscuits/c6v6/56fc0f760cf2c25af4c81c02.

2. J. E. Hurtgen Jr., "An Interview with Philip Yancey," *Relevant*, November 1, 2006, http://www.relevantmagazine.com/god/deeper-walk/features/1171 -an-interview-with-philip-yancey.

3. Haddon W. Robinson, *Jesus' Blueprint for Prayer* (Grand Rapids, MI: Our Daily Bread Ministries, 2016), 11–12.

CHAPTER 18: LET GOD LOVE YOU

1. Brennan Manning, *The Ragamuffin Gospel: Good News for the Bedraggled, Beat-Up, and Burnt Out* (Colorado Springs: Multnomah, 1990), 90.

2. Philip Yancey, *What's So Amazing about Grace?* (Grand Rapids, MI: Zondervan, 1997), 69.

CHAPTER 19: GETTING OUTSIDE OF YOURSELF

1. Quoted by The Dead Body That Claims It Isn't in "The Dead Collector" skit from the 1975 film, *Monty Python and the Holy Grail.*

2. See www.essentialcslewis.com/2015/09/12/experience-that-most-brutal.

3. Martin Luther King Jr., "The Drum Major Instinct," sermon, February 4, 1968, http://kingencyclopedia.stanford.edu/encyclopedia/documentsentry /doc_the_drum_major_instinct.

4. Adrian Gostick and Chester Elton, *The Carrot Principle: How the Best Managers Use Recognition to Engage Their People, Retain Talent, and Accelerate Performance* (New York: Free Press, 2007), 7–14.

CHAPTER 20: WORDS DO MATTER

1. @jimgaffigan, Twitter, 1:30 p.m., August 16, 2016, https://twitter.com /jimgaffigan/status/765616733327618048.

2. James Baldwin, *Notes of a Native Son* (Boston: Beacon Press, 2012), 103.

3. Philip Yancey, "Homosexuality," *PhilipYancey.com*, http://philipyancey .com/q-and-a-topics/homosexuality.

4. C. S. Lewis, *Mere Christianity*, rev. & enlarged ed. (New York: HarperOne, 2015), 123–24.

5. Mark Mitchell, "Are We Addicted to Negative Words?" *PreachingToday.com*, accessed October 25, 2016, http://preachingtoday.com/illustrations/2014 /june/6060914.html

6. Martin Luther King Jr., *Where Do We Go From Here* (New York: Harper & Row, 1967).

7. *Booker T. Washington Quotes*, http://www.literatureproject.com/booker-t -washington/booker-t-washington-quotes.htm.

CHAPTER 21: SOUNDS OF SILENCE

1. Frederick William Faber as quoted in *The Westminster Collection of Christian Quotations*, Martin H. Manser, ed. (Louisville: Westminster John Knox Press, 2001), 144.

2. Daniel A. Gross, "This Is Your Brain on Silence," *Nautilus*, August 21, 2014, http://nautil.us/issue/16/nothingness/this-is-your-brain-on-silence.

3. A. W. Tozer, *And He Dwelt Among Us: Teachings from the Gospel of John* (Ventura, CA: Regal, 2009), 88.

AFTERWORD: THE BEST PRESENT YOU CAN GIVE

1. Zig Ziglar, Facebook entry, posted April 12, 2014, https://www.facebook .com/ZigZiglar/photos/a.10150383579167863.372153.163583187862 /10152337531967863/?type=1&theater.

2. Dave Burchett, *Stay* (Carol Stream, IL: Tyndale, 2015), 21–22.

About the Author

DAVE BURCHETT is a successful television sports director with experiences that include the Olympic Games as well as professional and collegiate sports. Dave directed television coverage of Texas Rangers baseball for more than thirty years. During his career, he has earned a national Emmy and two local Emmys. He is the author of *Stay: Lessons My Dogs Taught Me about Life, Loss, and Grace*; *When Bad Christians Happen to Good People*; and *Bring 'Em Back Alive*. Dave enjoys speaking to churches and groups, and he blogs regularly at DaveBurchett.com. Dave and his wife, Joni, have three grown sons, several grandchildren, and another rescued Lab.

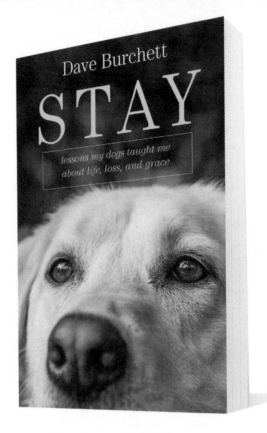

CHAPTER I

PUPPY LOVE

There is no psychiatrist in the world like a puppy licking your face.

~BEN WILLIAMS

My wife, Joni, and I are dog lovers. I grew up with a rescued mutt named Penny. She resembled some sort of mad scientist's terrier creation, and she was my best friend from elementary school until college. Here I am (pictured on the left) with Penny.

Joni loved and grew up in south florida with a sweet Boxer named Dutchess. Joni and Dutchess made life miserable for the local duck population by chasing them every day.

Dogs have always been a part of our lives. As 2002 approached, Joni and I were at that tough crossroads for every dog owner, facing the decision about what to do when a dog is near the end of its journey. Charlie, our nearly fourteen-year-old golden retriever, was fast approaching that moment. The winter of 2001, he teetered on barely functioning hips which made walking painful.

He was a far cry from the Charlie-is-a-handful years, which is a very kind way of saying he was crazy. Charlie was the perfect blend of alpha-dog testosterone and faithful friend for a household with three rambunctious boys. He ran, chased, wrestled, swam, dived, and cuddled with our sons Matt, Scott, and Brett. Charlie was their buddy through puberty and high school frustrations, much as Penny had served that role with me.

Other than breed differences, there was one other huge difference between Penny and Charlie. Remember Marley, the yellow Lab of book and movie fame, who was described as the world's worst dog? Well, Charlie certainly had to be in the conversation at eighty pounds of hard-charging destruction.

Charlie was particularly psychotic during thunderstorms, causing hundreds of dollars of damage to our home. If a storm hit while we were away, we entered the house with fear and trembling upon returning, afraid to see what Charlie had wrought. One time he chewed off a cabinet door in order to wedge himself under the sink. While he was hidden, he chewed off the sink trap, just to keep his mind off of the booms of the raging storm.

Another memorable time, we discovered our guinea pig's cage ripped apart and its former inhabitant, Squeakers, ominously missing. We feared the worst but found no *CSI: Rodent Edition* evidence of foul play. After a few hours we heard Squeakers's terrified call from underneath a built-in cabinet. Somehow Squeakers had squeezed her brown, black, and white fur-covered frame through a narrow opening to escape thunder-crazed Charlie. No amount of coaxing or food could get that trembling critter to come out of her refuge. She was too far back to reach in and pull her out. Finally, we hired a carpenter to saw a hole in the bottom of the cabinet so Squeakers could be saved.

Then there was the security breach incident. We were away from home when I received a surprise phone call from our security company that an alarm had been triggered. I was worried about the house but also wondered, *Is Charlie okay?* The local police showed up and reported seeing only a tail-wagging and very happy-to-see-anyone golden retriever who, upon further investigation, turned out to be the perp in the caper. In another fit of storm jitters, he had chewed through some wires.

I think you get the picture: Charlie did not handle life's storms well.

Still, in that odd paradigm that only dog people understand, we loved him dearly.

Matt and Scott were off to Baylor University at this time and youngest son, Brett, was just a couple of years away from leaving the nest. With Charlie's failing health, we wondered what our lives would look like without a dog around the house. Should we even consider the scenario of another dog? Perhaps it would be a welcome respite, not worrying about boarding a pet when we traveled or to be able to go out without concerns about what might await us when we got home.

That January, Scott called from school and got right to the point. His girlfriend (now his wife), Caroline, had "inherited" a Labrador puppy that had been passed around the dorm to several foster volunteers. The fun of having a cute puppy on campus had turned into a time-consuming reality: caring for a puppy is not far removed from caring for a baby. Knowing Charlie's condition, Scott and Caroline proposed that Joni and I take her—for a while. Scott hit the most vulnerable and by far weakest link in the family line of canine defense.

Me.

"Caroline has adopted this puppy temporarily. Her name is Hannah. We can't watch her this weekend. Could you keep her until we can find her a home?"

Within minutes of Hannah's arrival at our house, it was obvious that this puppy was going nowhere. She wasn't an ordinary Lab; her coat's color was not the usual light yellow Lab hue. She was a Fox Red Labrador, with the darker reddish tint. They are generally pricey little pups so, in retrospect, it was an added bonus to acquire her for free.

Over the next few weeks, it was clear that this puppy was something special. She had eyes that seemed to look into your soul. Her friendly expression was true to her character and she was more than happy to accommodate anyone who wanted to play at any time. Her ears were as soft as mink. Hannah was a keeper.

From the beginning, she instinctively knew that Charlie could not handle the aggressive play of a puppy. They became instant friends and Hannah was gentle with old guy Charlie in his final days.

I am a TV sports director for the Texas Rangers, which means I am on the road for about half of the baseball season from April through September. In April, I was in New York, working at Yankee Stadium, when Joni called with trembling voice to say she was taking Charlie to the vet for the last visit. He could no longer walk and refused to eat. His once unstoppable body was failing. It was time to say good-bye.

After I hung up, I saw a New York cop outside the stadium with his Labrador police dog at his side. Seeing that sweet Lab hit me hard; I was already missing my crazy friend Charlie. I approached the officer and asked him if I could pet the dog.

"He's working," the officer snapped at me.

"I understand, sir. I was just feeling sad. We had to say good-bye to our fourteen-year-old golden retriever today."

The cop's face immediately softened as he looked at me.

"Pet the dog."

"It's okay, officer. I understand that the dog is . . ."

"PET THE DOG."

"Yes, sir."

The power of this unique relationship we forge with our dogs is truly universal.

We had said good-bye to a dear friend. But God had given us a special gift named Hannah.

The heartwarming true tale of an irrepressible donkey who needed a home —and forever changed a family.

978-1-4143-9783-2 (Hardcover)
978-1-4143-9784-9 (Softcover)

When Rachel Anne Ridge discovered a wounded, frightened donkey standing in her driveway, she couldn't turn him away. And against all odds, he turned out to be the very thing her family needed most. They let him into their hearts . . . and he taught them things they never knew about life, love, and faith.

Prepare to fall in love with Flash: a quirky, unlikely hero with gigantic ears, a deafening bray, a personality as big as Texas, and a story you'll never forget.

Available everywhere books are sold.

Online Discussion *guide*

TAKE *your* TYNDALE READING EXPERIENCE *to the* NEXT LEVEL

A FREE discussion guide for this book is available at bookclubhub.net, perfect for sparking conversations in your book group or for digging deeper into the text on your own.

www.bookclubhub.net

You'll also find free discussion guides for other Tyndale books, e-newsletters, e-mail devotionals, virtual book tours, and more!